Picturing: Description and Illusion
in the Nineteenth-Century Novel

Picturing: Description and Illusion in the Nineteenth-Century Novel

MICHAEL IRWIN

Senior Lecturer in English, University of Kent

London
GEORGE ALLEN & UNWIN
Boston   Sydney

First published in 1979

GEORGE ALLEN & UNWIN LTD
40 Museum Street, London WC1A 1LU

© George Allen & Unwin (Publishers) Ltd, 1979

British Library Cataloguing in Publication Data

Irwin, Michael
  Picturing.
  1. English fiction – 19th century – History and
  criticism 2. Description (Rhetoric)
  I. Title
  823′.8′0022   PR830.D/   78–40883

  ISBN 0–04–801021–0

Typeset in 10 on 11 point Baskerville by Trade Linotype Ltd, Birmingham
and printed in Great Britain
by Hollen Street Press, Slough, Berkshire

Preface

This book concerns the attempts made by the great nineteenth-century novelists to stir the reader's visual imagination – to make him picture the people and places described. In short, it concerns what Henry James called 'solidity of specification'. My intention was to produce a work a good deal more pragmatic and technical than most academic studies of the novel. The writer of realistic fiction, as he works from page to page, from sentence to sentence, is repeatedly confronted by the problems of what, when and how to describe. Should this character's face be sketched? Should that one be given a suit of clothes? Should the room they sit in be furnished? If the answer to any of these questions is 'yes', how is the task to be effectively and economically accomplished? In this area of craftsmanship the novelists of the nineteenth century surely learned a great deal from one another, both consciously and unconsciously. Certain techniques soon became widespread; certain conventions were established. But within those conventions there was scope for a wide variety of emphasis and effect. To investigate the descriptive habits of the major Victorian novelists is greatly to enhance one's understanding of the workings of their fiction.

My aim has been to present, not a single thesis, but a family of arguments and speculations that should, I hope, prove individually interesting and mutually reinforcing. I have alternated between theoretical discussion and detailed analysis of particular novels. If this book is persuasive I hope that it might modify, to some extent, conventional academic views about realist fiction in general, and about certain famous specific novels. What I would like to have achieved is to have provided the scholar and the student with an additional critical tool, an additional way of looking at fiction. The best critic can do no more than make us consciously aware of virtues in a work of literature that have previously passed unnoticed or unappreciated. The descriptive skills that I am principally concerned with have always constituted a powerfully influential aspect of fiction, but they have been very little studied. They tend to slip through the mesh of established critical procedures. The student is trained to consider characterisation, symbolism, structure, tone, and so on, but is rarely asked to analyse the means by which an author has involved him sensually, as well as intellectually, in a novel.

There are two main reasons, I think, for this neglect. Academic criticism tends to be strongly analogical in tendency : procedures appropriate to one period or genre are regularly appropriated for the exploration of subjects to which they are less relevant. Since neither poetry nor drama involves anything usefully comparable with the descriptive aspect of realistic fiction, that aspect has been insufficiently studied. But still more to the point is the methodological problem. The material concerned is scattered, miscellaneous, often fragmentary – altogether immensely resistant to codification. In setting about my task I found that I was obliged to make a number of bluntly arbitrary decisions in the interests of clarity, coherence, and decent brevity. I limited myself as far as possible to the Victorian period. I decided, reluctantly, to make only brief reference to Continental fiction. To achieve reasonably clear-cut chapter-division I created a number of artificial categories – 'Faces', 'Clothes', and so on – which I proceeded to abuse. Faces, of course, are inseparable from Bodies, and Bodies tend to be Clothed. The only motive and justification for this categorising was that it made discussion manageable. I did not attempt to produce a balanced account of the period. It seemed more sensible to work with the materials that were presented by my instinctive preferences and accidental reading patterns. If anyone chooses to fill in some of the large gaps that I have left, I will be only too pleased. It was less the omission of particular authors than of particular themes that I regretted. For the sake of economy I abandoned projected chapters on Meals, Weather and Landscape.

Because I was obliged to deal in numerous brief quotations my discussion became very cluttered. Eventually it seemed a good idea to remove a large proportion of these quotations from the text proper, and prefix them to the relevant chapters as a kind of introduction or prologue. My interest in the technical problems concerned is such that I would cheerfully read an entire anthology of these descriptive extracts; but I'm aware that this is likely to be regarded as an eccentric taste. I hope, all the same, that each set of quotations will be read thoughtfully as part of my argument, and not merely skimmed, or dismissed, as a conglomeration of epigraphs. Each of the extracts has been chosen with some care. The selection and the juxtaposition imply themes and possibilities that I do not always pursue explicitly in the text. I rely on the reader to read between the quotations.

The fact that I was usually dealing with very simple materials and techniques created a number of difficulties. Quite often I felt that I was being obliged to spell out the obvious, or to traverse familiar ground. I hope that when I do so it is always as a means towards saying something new. Conversely there were times when I feared that a certain argument, or stage of an argument, must seem disproportionately abstract and complex in relation to the passages that I was discussing. Central to this study is the belief that in fiction simple descriptive devices can produce very complex effects. To make my point I was obliged to run the risk of producing occasional strained or trite passages.

Since I had to quote innumerable snippets from a great many novels there was a danger that each page would be thigh-deep in footnotes. In the end it seemed wiser to have virtually none. The decision was the easier in that there were very few critical works that I wished to quote, since so few critics have worked this area. John Carey and Barbara Hardy, in books that I refer to in the text, have said some relevant things, and so has John Harvey in *Victorian Novelists and Their Illustrators.* In terms of viewpoint and method the nearest approach that I have seen to what I am attempting is an article that Anthony Burgess published in *The Times Literary Supplement* some six years ago. All these works deal in descriptive or technical minutiae, and all of them have the virtue of being entertaining. That coincidence suggests how much of our pleasure in Victorian fiction resides in detail, in things, in the grain of the story-telling.

MICHAEL IRWIN
University of Kent

Contents

Picturing: Description and Illusion in the Nineteenth-Century Novel

Chapter 1

Introduction

One can speak best from one's own taste, and I may therefore venture to say that the air of reality (solidity of specification) seems to me to be the supreme virtue of a novel – the merit on which all its other merits . . . helplessly and submissively depend. If it be not there they are all as nothing, and if these be there, they owe their effect to the success with which the author has produced the illusion of life. . . . It is here in very truth that he competes with life; it is here that he competes with his brother the painter in *his* attempt to render the look of things, the look that conveys their meaning, to catch the colour, the relief, the expression, the surface, the substance of the human spectacle. . . . All life solicits him, and to 'render' the simplest surface, to produce the most momentary illusion, is a very complicated business.

Henry James, The Art of Fiction

But may I not be forgiven for thinking it a wonderful testimony to my being made for my art, that when, in the midst of this trouble and pain, I sit down to my book, some beneficent power shows it all to me, and tempts me to be interested, and I don't invent it – really do not – *but see it*, and write it down. . . .

Charles Dickens, Letter to Forster

It is so that I have lived with my characters, and thence has come whatever success I have attained. There is a gallery of them, and of all in that gallery I may say that I know the tone of the voice, and the colour of the hair, every flame of the eye, and the very clothes they wear. Of each man I could assert whether he would have said these or the other words; of every woman, whether she would then have smiled or so have frowned.

Anthony Trollope, Autobiography

Here Mr Tulliver put his stick between his legs, and took out
his snuff-box, for the greater enjoyment of this anecdote, which
dropped from him in fragments, as if he every other moment
lost narration in vision.

George Eliot, *The Mill on the Floss*

' He saw everything he related. It passed before him, as he spoke,
so vividly, that in the intensity of his earnestness, he presented
what he described to me, with greater distinctness than I can
express.

Charles Dickens, *David Copperfield*

Merely corroborative detail, intended to give artistic verisimilitude to an otherwise bald and unconvincing narrative.

W. S. Gilbert, *The Mikado*

I

Nineteenth-century fiction is full of attempts to make the reader
see what is taking place. Some of them involve minute description
– of faces, for example, or clothes, or furniture, or streets. Some are
mere stage directions, indicating how a character moves, speaks,
reacts. The object of this study is to examine the part played by
such material in the novel in general, and in the over-all economy
of particular novels. Why are these passages included? What sort
of work do they do? How much do they matter? Which authors
make them most telling? Could it be meaningful to claim that a
given novel contains too many or too few of them?

This is a crucial aspect of the novelist's art, because it has so
much to do with imaginative energy. Detail of this kind not only
stimulates the reader to visualise, but can also seem to demonstrate
that the writer himself has visualised intensely. Dickens and
Trollope are two of many novelists to claim that the scenes and
characters which they invent are directly perceived by them. What
Dickens imagines, he sees, and what he sees, he describes. The three
processes are almost inseparable. *David Copperfield* provides an
especially clear example of the Dickensian method, since the
narrator's explicit intention is to re-experience his past, and so put
it vividly before the reader. David's account of his childhood drifts
naturally into the present tense : 'Here is a long passage. . . . Here
is our pew in the church. . . . And now I see the outside of our
house. . . . Now I am in the garden at the back. . . .' When an
episode is particularly significant, as when David hears of his
mother's death, his attempt to project himself and his readers among
the very actualities of the scene involves a fierce concentration of
sensual detail :

How well I recollect the kind of day it was! I smell the fog that hung about the place; I see the hoar frost, ghostly, through it; I feel my rimy hair fall clammy on my cheek; I look along the dim perspective of the schoolroom, with a sputtering candle here and there to light up the foggy morning, and the breath of the boys wreathing and smoking in the raw cold as they blow upon their fingers, and tap their feet upon the floor.

In such passages the narrator is, so to speak, getting back inside his own skin, and inviting us to see, feel and smell with him. But David's apparent vividness of recollection is really, of course, his creator's vividness of invention. In the Preface to *Dombey and Son* Dickens remarks: 'I know, in my fancy, every stair in the little midshipman's house, and could swear to every pew in the church in which Florence was married, or to every young gentleman's bedstead in Doctor Blimber's establishment. . . .' The claim will not seem wildly extravagant to the admirer of his novels. Repeatedly they imply this immediacy of perception, though only the first-person narratives can boast it explicitly:

The incident is so impressed on my remembrance, that if I were a draughtsman I could draw its form here, I dare say, accurately as it was that day, and little Em'ly springing forward to her destruction (as it appeared to me), with a look that I have never forgotten, directed far out to sea.

As plainly as I behold what happened, I will try to write it down. I do not recall it, but see it done; for it happens again before me.

It may be that such assertions as these are really part of an attempt to achieve the imaginative command that they describe: Dickens is helping and forcing himself to picture a scene by stating that he already sees it. But clearly he does visualise his stories with extraordinary distinctness, and is concerned to make his readers respond at the same level of intensity.

A similar, if rather less clear-cut, case could be made out for nearly all Dickens's contemporaries or near-contemporaries – most obviously, perhaps, for Hardy, Eliot and Gaskell. Indeed, such a case will be implied in the chapters that follow. It was natural for the novelists of the period to see, or at least try to see, the stories that they composed. But my immediate point concerns the likely product of this imaginative grasp, which is a corresponding degree of conviction on the part of the reader. Most of us will accept readily enough that a character in any sort of tale is 'real'. We 'believe in' Bulldog Drummond, or Billy Bunter, or Dan Archer – but only in a trivial sense. A major feat of the developed realistic novel was to make a character, a scene, an environment believable in a far ampler way, partly by providing more to believe in, partly through greater power and skill of presentation. But academic critics rarely make any attempt to assess the likely strength of the reader's conviction or involvement. The question is a highly subjective one, and is further confused by the fact that the energies and the techniques concerned, or something very like them, can be found in a number of best-selling works, lacking any serious fictional purpose. But it sometimes seems to me that the issue is disposed of altogether, by a Knight's fork of critical appraisal. If a novel is deemed to be 'minor', imaginative vigour and sharpness of description are not taken to offer significant compensation, and hence acquire the status of incidental merits only. But a 'major' work is assumed, as it were by definition, to have achieved suitable standards of vividness and substantiality. Critical attention is deflected to character, theme, structure. Such a novel can virtually cease to be judged by the practical criteria that a reviewer would apply to a newly published work. The academic commentator may not admit, may not even notice, that certain episodes have been inadequately imagined or ineptly recorded. Conversely, scenes which have an unusual force of a purely descriptive kind are liable to be under-praised, or to be praised for the wrong reasons.

This necessarily generalised argument may appear superficial and unpersuasive as it stands. I hope that the detailed analyses of which this book is largely to be composed will both elucidate it and give it weight.

II

Imaginative intensity on the author's part by no means guarantees 'solidity of specification'. This study will be very much concerned with the technical skills necessary to transform the former into the latter. The novelist's task is far from being merely a matter of transcribing his crowding mental images. Most teachers of creative writing will have encountered the student who carries in his head a scene powerfully real to him, but proves quite unable to commun-icate it. Even if he has a good eye and a decent command of language, there are problems of selection, ordering, pace and balance that can seem insuperable.

The great Victorian novelists usually had a great deal of scene-painting to do, either because, like Dickens, they were imaginatively prolific, or because, like Eliot or Gissing, they believed strongly in the formative and restrictive power of the social milieu, and hence saw potential significance even in minor physical aspects of the environment. Their works are full of descriptive set-pieces, many of which have been justly praised. But the real technical challenge lay elsewhere, in reconciling description with action. The extended set-piece is, in its very nature, static. It may provide a relevant prelude to a dramatised scene, but it can scarcely be accommodated within one. Victorian fiction, of course, was largely made up of such dramatised scenes, and these required, in any case, a rather different visual life of their own. The reader who has been made to see the drawing-room of a great house will expect also to see the faces and movements of the characters who quarrel in that drawing-room. The novelist must interfuse dialogue and description, prompt ear and eye alternately, since he cannot do so simultaneously. Many a fictional scene owes its vitality largely to the skill with which the author has deployed a variety of brief hints or reminders; and it is a skill that has tended to elude critical inquiry.

Two related issues must be mentioned at this point. One is the question of imaginative consistency. Numerous novelists have the power of conveying the appearance of a particular person, room or street. Far fewer prove capable of sustaining their own, and hence their readers', sense of that appearance. It can be an intricate task, because even the most vigorous descriptive set-piece creates only a temporary impression. A 600-page novel makes great demands on the reader : there is such a diversity of information to comprehend, to interpret, to cross-relate. One episode or character crowds out another. The description of the heroine's uncle, in Chapter 2, will surely be forgotten by the time he reappears in Chapter 12. It is for the author to supply some appropriate reminders. And this he is unlikely to do unless the character has remained clearly and consistently present to him. It is a truth too little acknowledged that much of a novelist's authority derives from his ability to establish that the characters and settings he has imagined have definition and permanency in his own mind.

The further, and disheartening, complication is the fact that descriptive writing, of whatever mode or quality, must be uncertain in its effects, since so much depends on the responsiveness of the reader. Clearly in absolute terms description is impossible. One could not verbally convey an adequate idea of a tree to a man who had never come across one. The novelist can persuade his readers to see only what they are capable of seeing. He cannot transmit to them an exact picture of the pretty face or the frosty landscape that he sees with his mind's eye. His aim must be to stimulate them into visualising aptly and intensely for themselves. It follows that he should not concentrate exclusively on producing a faithful record of his own imaginings. His true end product is not the printed page, but the illusion created in the reader's mind.

I take this to be an irritatingly elusive and abstract notion, from the point of view of either novelist or critic; but its practical implications are plain enough. 'Solidity of specification' is not simply a matter of close observation and faithful description of 'the look of things'. The novelist must come to terms with the requirements and limitations of his medium, and with the probable expectations and responses of his readers. Like 'his brother the painter' he must master a whole range of technical skills, including selection, exaggeration, repetition, foreshortening, equivalence, juxtaposition.

Criticism of the novel has in general been pretty remote from the practicalities of *writing* fiction. It is often noted that a given scene 'comes alive', or that a given novelist has a visual imagination. But there have been few inquiries into the nature of the sleights and techniques by which 'the air of reality' may be achieved. When at work the writer is likely to be less occupied with the larger issues of theme or characterisation than with such page-to-page problems as establishing that his hero has a certain type of face, or keeping the reader reminded that a certain conversation takes place over the dinner-table or in a moonlit garden. The effects involved may be far from insignificant. Many a striking scene in fiction owes its sense of place, or atmosphere, or physical reality to a few brief descriptive sentences, shrewdly placed. This is high art, well worth analysis.

In matters of this kind – matters of nuts and bolts – novelists can and do learn from one another. Would-be novelists might profitably make a systematic investigation of such techniques. Art students analyse and copy famous works partly in order to develop their own creative skills. There seems to be no reason why novels should not be examined for the same purpose. Since one of the objectives of this book is, in fact, to relate the academic study of fiction to the technicalities of composition, I hope that it might be of some use to courses in creative writing as well as to courses in English literature. Many commentators on the novel seem to see the novelist himself as a detached unerring creator, dispensing here an irony, there an insight, everywhere meaning and metaphor. For the purposes of this particular work I prefer to picture him at his desk, pen in hand, frowning anxiously over a half-finished sentence.

III

A basic purpose of the kind of material I am concerned with is to authenticate and vivify the story. But insensibly and inevitably it becomes part of the *meaning* of that story. This can be a deliberate effect. Often, for example, fragments of description, through a process of displacement, are made a means of conveying insights into the emotions or the psychology of a given character. A man's face, or clothes, or possessions reveal his personality. Landscape or weather reflects his mood. Such devices are familiar enough; but there are less obvious ways in which 'corroborative detail' can acquire cumulative significance. In presenting any scene the novelist is obliged to select from the infinitude of circumstances that would be attendant on a comparable situation in real life. He may or may not choose to describe the season, the weather, the light, the scenery, the protagonist's face, physique, gestures, tones of voice, the sounds and smells of the environment, and so on. Naturally the elements selected are those the writer takes to be important in terms of the meaning of his scene as he has conceived it. A similar process, operating over his novel as a whole, can come to imply what aspects of life itself he feels to be most important. Whether he intends it or not, the inclusion of certain kinds of information and the exclusion of certain other kinds suggest some of his essential beliefs. The virtual absence of description of any sort – as in a small number of notable nineteenth-century novels – is in itself expressive.

Since a novelist's general habit of description is spontaneous and instinctive, the process of self-disclosure that I am describing is likely to be outside his conscious control. Ideally, of course, the ostensible meanings of his narrative should be happily reinforced by these involuntary affirmations. But instinct and intellect do not always pull together. At an extreme the configuration of incidental detail can suggest a subversive meaning, bluntly hostile to the author's explicit intentions.

A wide range of the techniques and tendencies outlined above will be illustrated, in the chapters that follow, through close study of particular novels. The discrepancy of scale between the causes and effects I am concerned with is so great that my argument can only be made persuasive, or even, perhaps, fully intelligible, in relation to specific examples. General discussion is also constrained by the fact that, as regards descriptive method and scope, any individual work is likely to be, in some sense, a special case – because it is narrated in the first person, for example, or because it is set abroad, or in the past. It is especially important to the kind of analysis I shall be attempting that each text should be approached very distinctly on its own terms. But there is, none the less, an important general argument that I hope these separate studies will serve to enforce. Conventional critical procedures seem to me quite often to produce a misleading account of the meaning or the workings of a given novel, because they attach so much emphasis to indications on, or very near, the surface of the text. I hope that the analytical exercises that I attempt will cumulatively demonstrate how much of the energy and essential meaning of a work of fiction may reside in what Gilbert called 'corroborative detail' and Henry James called 'stuff'.

It isn't surprising that criticism should have taken a long time to begin to come to terms with 'stuff'. Until the invention of the novel there was really very little of it in literature. If some mundane 'thing' found its way into a poetic or dramatic context it would be for a readily comprehensible special effect, as with Lear's 'Pray you, undo this button'. But nineteenth-century fiction is crammed with things of every possible kind : furniture, crockery, cutlery, toys, pictures, tools, bird-cages, busts, walking-sticks, jewellery, watches, thimbles. In minor novels, it is true, such properties may amount to no more than lumber; but in serious works they can and do contribute to a great range of effects. For example, they, too, can help to establish the authority of the writer. Over a whole narrative the diversity of the objects that he mentions or describes will imply the breadth of his experience. The novelist, like the writer of epic, has an interest in asserting his qualifications to tell a story by demonstrating how much he has seen, or done, or learned. It is impossible to read a novel by Dickens without becoming consciously or unconsciously aware that the author is a man who has cooked a meal, cleaned his own shoes, visited prisons and pawn-shops, travelled by coach, train and ship, played with children. . . . The list would make no clear sense unless drawn out to absurd length; but the general idea, I hope, has been at least faintly indicated. Certain episodes or characters become the more plausible, interesting or striking because we feel them to be the creation of a writer of proven knowledge, experience, sympathy.

Again, a quality of major literature in general is its capacity to point to relationships between aspects of experience that the reader has never previously connected. But the novel is peculiarly rich in effects of this kind because it can effortlessly incorporate reference to so immense a variety of sights, sounds, objects, smells, textures. The very simplicity of the process, however, poses severe problems of control. Many a mildly gifted writer can achieve surprising juxtapositions, or suggest unexpected correspondences, but only spasmodically, through chance insight. The very density of these isolated moments can show up a thinness elsewhere. But the connections that the great novelist makes explicit seem to imply, and to derive from, an entire system of inter-relationship within a given work. The moments of perception disclose a habit of vision.

There is a further potentiality in the 'stuff' of fiction which I perhaps cannot describe briefly without sounding pretentious. The novel can register a great many small diurnal pleasures that are not recorded in most literary modes. Captain Cuttle cooking dinner, Tess milking a cow, Adam Bede planing a plank, Squire Hamley and his son taking a pipe together are all, regardless of the larger drama to which these activities are incidental, displaying a positive aspect of life. Through such interludes the realistic novel can come to precipitate a curious and original kind of comedy, an implicit optimism sometimes powerful enough to subvert an ostensible pessimism.

I hope I have said enough in this section to suggest that the theoretical ramifications of my subject could be exceedingly complex. At several points I have been tempted to codify, to cramp a suggestive generalisation into a compact theory. These temptations I have resisted. For reasons that I hope will sufficiently emerge, this seems to me an area of investigation in which to codify would be to falsify. My discussion will be led outwards in a number of different directions, but it will constantly revert from the more abstract issues to practicalities of technique, to specific topics, specific novels, specific passages.

Chapter 2

Fictitious Faces

. . . his face was, at least, half a yard in length, brown and shrivelled, with projecting cheek-bones, little grey eyes on the greenish hue, a large hook-nose, a pointed chin, a mouth from ear to ear, very ill furnished with teeth, and a high, narrow forehead, well furrowed with wrinkles.

Tobias Smollett, *Humphry Clinker*

I see her now. Thin in face and figure, sallow in complexion, regular in features, with perfect teeth, lips like a thread, a large, prominent chin, a well-opened, but frozen eye, of light at once craving and ingrate.

Charlotte Brontë, *Villette*

'Hah! Good day, age about forty, height about five feet nine, black hair, generally rather handsome visage, complexion dark, eyes dark, thin long and sallow face, aquiline nose, but not straight, having a peculiar inclination towards the left cheek which imparts a sinister expression! Good day, one and all!'

Charles Dickens, *A Tale of Two Cities*

Mr Dempster habitually held his chin tucked in, and his head hanging forward, weighed down, perhaps, by a preponderant occiput, and a bulging forehead, between which his closely-clipped coronal surface lay like a flat and new-mown table-land. The only other observable features were puffy cheeks and a protruding yet lipless mouth. Of his nose I can only say that it was snuffy; and as Mr Dempster was never caught in the act of looking at anything in particular, it would have been difficult to swear to the colour of his eyes.

George Eliot, *Scenes of Clerical Life*

Studying her features, he saw how fine was their expression. The prominent forehead, with its little unevenness that meant brains; the straight eyebrows, strongly marked, with deep vertical furrows generally drawn between them; the chestnut-brown eyes, with long lashes; the high-bridged nose, thin and delicate; the intellectual lips, a protrusion of the lower one, though very slight, marking itself when he caught her profile; the big, strong chin; the shapely neck – why, after all, it was a kind of beauty.

George Gissing, *The Odd Women*

'He has red hair, very red, close-curling, and a pale face, long in shape, with straight, good features and little, rather queer whiskers that are as red as his hair. His eyebrows are, somehow, darker; they look particularly arched and as if they might move a good deal. His eyes are sharp, strange – awfully; but I only know clearly that they're rather small and very fixed. His mouth's wide, and his lips are thin, and except for his little whiskers he's quite clean-shaven. He gives me a sort of sense of looking like an actor.'

Henry James, *The Turn of the Screw*

'How can one describe a man? I can give you an inventory: heavy eyebrows, dark eyes, a straight nose, thick dark hair, large white hands – and – let me see – oh, an exquisite cambric pocket handkerchief.'

George Eliot, *Middlemarch*

But to attempt to gain a view of her – or indeed of any fascinating woman – from a measured category, is as difficult as to appreciate . . . a full chord of music by piping the notes in succession.

Thomas Hardy, *Desperate Remedies*

Attempts at description are stupid: who can all at once describe a human being? Even when he is presented to us we only begin that knowledge of his appearance which must be completed by innumerable impressions under differing circumstances. We recognise the alphabet; we are not sure of the language.

George Eliot, *Daniel Deronda*

This Woman was not very amiable in her Person. Whether she sat to my Friend *Hogarth*, or no, I will not determine; but she exactly resembled the young Woman who is pouring out her Mistress's Tea in the third Picture of the Harlot's Progress.

Henry Fielding, *Tom Jones*

Those who remember Greuze's 'Head of a Girl', have an idea of Cytherea's look askance at the turning.

Thomas Hardy, *Desperate Remedies*

Having come more into the open he could now be seen rising against the sky, his profile appearing on the light background like the portrait of a gentleman in black cardboard. It assumed the form of a low-crowned hat, an ordinary-shaped nose, an ordinary chin, an ordinary neck, and ordinary shoulders.

Thomas Hardy, *Under the Greenwood Tree*

. . . a girl whose appearance you could not characterise except by saying that her figure was slight and of middle stature, her features small, her eyes tolerable and her complexion sallow. . . .

George Eliot, *Daniel Deronda*

He says to himself that novelists, by a too exact description of their characters, hinder the reader's imagination rather than help it, and that they ought to allow each individual to picture their personages to himself according to his own fancy.

André Gide, *The Counterfeiters*

To conceive this right, – call for pen and ink – here's a paper ready to your hand. – Sit down, Sir, paint her to your mind – as like your mistress as you can – as unlike your wife as your conscience will let you – 'tis all one to me – please but your own fancy in it.

Laurence Sterne, *Tristram Shandy*

There's no art
To find the mind's construction in the face . . .

William Shakespeare, *Macbeth*

A profile was visible against the dull monochrome of cloud around her; and it was as though side shadows from the features of Sappho and Mrs Siddons had converged upwards from the tomb to form an image like neither but suggesting both. This, however, was mere superficiality. In respect of character a face may make certain admissions by its outline; but it fully confesses only in its changes. So much is this the case that what is called the play of the features often helps more in understanding a man or woman than the earnest labours of all the other members together.

Thomas Hardy, *The Return of the Native*

It was Miss Murdstone who was arrived, and a gloomy-looking lady she was; dark, like her brother . . . and with very heavy eyebrows, nearly meeting over her large nose, as if, being disabled by the wrongs of her sex from wearing whiskers, she had carried them to that account.

Charles Dickens, *David Copperfield*

. . . a chappie with no chin, and a moustache like a lady's eyebrow. . . .

Thomas Hardy, *Jude the Obscure*

She was a sallow, unhealthy, sweet-looking young woman with a careworn look. . . .

Elizabeth Gaskell, *Mary Barton*

He had hair that was very nearly black, and a clean-shaven face, best described, perhaps, as of bureaucratic type.

George Gissing, *New Grub Street*

A cheerful looking, merry boy, fresh with running home in the rain; fair-faced, bright-eyed, and curly-haired.

Charles Dickens, *Dombey and Son*

. . . a wooden-featured, blue-faced Major, with his eyes starting out of his head. . . .

Charles Dickens, *Dombey and Son*

. . . wiping his dull red and yellow face. . . .

Charles Dickens, *Little Dorrit*

Mr Benjamin Allen was a coarse, stout, thick-set young man, with black hair cut rather short, and a white face cut rather long.

Charles Dickens, *The Pickwick Papers*

'He is remarkably like the portrait of Locke. He has the same deep eye-sockets.'
'Had Locke those two white moles with hairs on them?'
'Oh, I daresay! when people of a certain sort looked at him,' said Dorothea, walking away a little.

George Eliot, *Middlemarch*

. . . from her boy's description and the casual words of the other milkers, Rhoda Brook could raise a mental image of the unconscious Mrs Lodge that was realistic as a photograph.

Thomas Hardy, *'The Withered Arm'*

My inward representation even of comparatively indifferent faces is so vivid as to make portraits of them unsatisfactory to me.

George Eliot, letter to Mrs Elma Stuart, 24 December 1879

Swithin was not in the habit of noticing people's features; he scarcely ever observed any detail of physiognomy in his friends, a generalisation from their whole aspect forming his idea of them. . . .

Thomas Hardy, *Two on a Tower*

To say, therefore, that a woman's eyes were blue, black, or brown, her hair red, black, or gold, her smile sweet and her voice musical conveys no image to the reader who, till then, was ignorant of the existence of the person so described, but if he knows a person whom the description resembles, then it is that person whom he sees and not the one which the writer beheld or had seen while he was trying to convey his impressions of her to another.

C. Moore, *The Twilight of Jibs and Topsails*

'I shouldn't know you again if we *did* meet,' Humpty Dumpty replied in a discontented tone, giving her one of his fingers to shake: 'you're so exactly like other people.'

'The face is what one goes by, generally,' Alice remarked in a thoughtful tone.

'That's just what I complain of,' said Humpty Dumpty. 'Your face is the same as everybody has – the two eyes, so –' (marking their places in the air with his thumb) 'nose in the middle, mouth under. It's always the same. Now if you had the two eyes on the same side of the nose, for instance – or the mouth at the top – that would be *some* help.'

Lewis Carroll, *Through the Looking-Glass*

I

Every major nineteenth-century novelist attempted physical descriptions of at least some of his characters – descriptions often so long and detailed as to suggest careful preparation. Their main purpose seems plain enough : to encourage and enable the reader to visualise the characters concerned, and to reveal something of their personality or temperament. Yet such passages have attracted little critical attention even as contributions to the full-scale psychological portrait. Commonly analysis of the characterisation of an Emma Woodhouse, a Dorothea Brooke or a Gabriel Oak takes no notice of the visual element in the portrayal. There are some exceptions to the general rule – for example, the minor characters of Dickens have necessarily to be discussed in terms of the physical data that go so far towards defining them – but on the whole the assumption seems to be that the visual aspect is of very little importance.

There are obvious reasons for our being less interested than nineteenth-century readers in this area of the novelist's technique. Few people nowadays would argue that the face is a particularly useful indicator of character, whereas many writers of the last century had at least a residual belief in physiognomy or phrenology. Since some of the greatest Victorian novels were published in serial form emphatic physical delineation became a helpful means of establishing a character in the reader's recollection through the weeks intervening between episodes. This function, of course, has lapsed. In any case it may be that we have grown so accustomed to an easy visual diet of photographs, films and television that the mind's eye has lost some of its ability to respond to the limited range of signals that a prose description of a face and figure can supply.

But the technical and critical issues involved are by no means obsolete and are unlikely to become so. Novelists continue to attempt, by direct or indirect means, to make their characters visualisable, and they encounter the same problems as their predecessors. From the point of view of the would-be describer human faces are dishearteningly alike in their general composition. The similarities are so much more obvious than the differences that the distinction between prettiness and plainness can well be a matter of a gramme or two of nostril or half a centimetre of lip. For the most part our facial apparatus is immobile and intrinsically inexpressive. We can wrinkle our foreheads, and in a trivial way our noses, and we can knit our brows. All other movement is confined to eyes and mouths. Complexions vary only through a narrow range of whitish pinks, and most British hair is an unclassifiable sub-species of brown. It is scarcely surprising that our apprehension of the faces we see is limited and impressionistic. To recall to a friend's mind the appearance of someone he knows quite well but is momentarily unable to 'place' can be an impossible task, unless there is some striking attribute in the case, such as red hair or a broken nose. The Identikit process, which has the advantage of working through visual rather than verbal equivalents, has shown itself to be extremely fallible. Not only are some faces more memorable or describable than others; it would seem also that the capacity to perceive and recall the significant details of someone else's appearance varies greatly from person to person. Many people – the reader can test himself on this point – are not consciously aware of the colour of their friends' eyes.

When such uncertainties are common in relation to real-life faces, then the question of our response to fictional portraits is bound to seem an elusive one. The writer may or may not have the habit, or knack, of visualising faces to himself. Even if he has, he must proceed to cope with the difficulties of verbal transcription. And the eventual reader, in his turn, may or may not happen to be of the visualising turn of mind. It seems likely that some readers would tend to corporealise, to invest with visual reality, a novel devoid of description, while others may possibly dematerialise, apprehend only in abstract terms, such physically detailed fiction as that of Hardy or Dickens.

There is much to be said, then, for what seems to be the tacitly accepted critical view that the subject is one that cannot be, and perhaps does not merit being, pursued far. The lack of useful terminology forces the most visual of novelists to resort to inert adjectives or downright cliché. Eyes are repeatedly 'bright', 'sparkling', 'dark' or 'deep'; lips are unsurprisingly 'red', teeth 'white', cheeks 'pink'. The feeblest of commercial story-tellers can put together some sort of portrait in these terms. Conversely certain major writers – Austen and James, for example – have preferred to supply only the most minimal indications of the appearance of their characters; yet this deficiency, where it has been evident, has not usually been regarded as a defect. In theory it seems that a writer's answer to the question 'What does your heroine look like?' might properly be : 'The question has no meaning – she isn't real.'

But manifestly the great nineteenth-century novelists would not have given such an answer. Again and again, if sometimes after preliminary caveats or disclaimers, they made their attempts at word-portraiture. If they could not be certain that the result would be the one they were hoping for, they were at least persuaded that *something* relevant would be achieved. It seems worthwhile to examine a number of these attempts and try to assess their effectiveness.

II

She was but a little thing; and it cannot be said of her . . . that she was a beauty. The charm of her face consisted in the peculiar, watery brightness of her eyes – in the corners of which it would always seem that a diamond of a tear was lurking whenever any matter of excitement was afoot. Her light-brown hair was soft and smooth and pretty. As hair it was very well, but it had no speciality. Her mouth was somewhat large, but full of every-varying expression. Her forehead was low and broad, with prominent temples, on which it was her habit to clasp tightly her little outstretched fingers, as she sat listening to you. . . .

What else can be said of her face or personal appearance that will interest a reader? When she smiled, there was the daintiest little dimple on her cheek. And when she laughed, that little nose, which was not as well-shaped a nose as it might have been, would almost change its shape and cock itself up in its mirth. Her hands were very thin and long, and so were her feet – by no

means models as were those of her friend Lady Eustace. She was
a little, thin, quick, graceful creature, whom it was impossible
that you should see without wishing to have near you.

The Eustace Diamonds

Trollope's description of Lucy Morris will be familiar in kind to the
reader of Victorian fiction – perhaps so familiar as to elicit an easy
unreflecting response. Yet it involves a number of assumptions that
are worth examining. He takes it for granted that we will *want* to
form a mental picture of the character after this fashion, that this
visual information 'will interest a reader'. The passage implies that
we see a new acquaintance as an aggregation of particular physical
features – in this case, hair, eyes, mouth, forehead, nose, dimple,
hands and feet. Trollope does not seem to doubt that such an
inventory can provide a stable means of communication, can enable
us to reassemble for ourselves the complete face and form that he
has imagined. He clearly anticipates that we will accept his verdict
as creator; will share his taste for watery eyes, and be favourably
influenced by the indulgent 'little', five times repeated.

But each of these assumptions, or conventions, is dubious. There
are some notable novels in which the physical appearance, even of
the hero, is left entirely undescribed : *Great Expectations* and *A
Portrait of the Artist as a Young Man* are examples. Most of us,
surely, neither see nor recall people in the way Trollope suggests –
the way of a portrait-painter or a policeman. And even if a picture
could be transmitted by these means, or something like them, it does
not follow that our reaction would be what Trollope expects. The
face and mannerisms that appeal to him might be unappealing to us.

Such comment might seem disproportionately solemn and
theoretical. After all, Trollope has one or two practical problems
to solve, and the passage in question is adequate to the purpose. He
needs to provide a description of Lucy Morris sufficiently emphatic
to keep her alive in the reader's memory through those considerable
passages of the novel in which she is to play no part. The nature of
her attractiveness must be defined with some precision : she must be
appealing enough, despite her comparative poverty, to win Frank
Greystock's love, but not so beautiful as to preclude the possibility
that Lady Eustace will eclipse her in his eyes. Various hints dropped
in the description become significant later. Frank Greystock himself thinks of Lucy as 'a little thing', and that estimation can
conveniently drift from affection to condescension : 'a humble little
thing'. If these general effects are satisfactorily achieved it might
seem pernickety to argue about small matters of tone or redundancy.

There is even a good case for seeing this loose and leisurely kind of introduction to a character as providing a useful opportunity that the twentieth-century writer has lost. To over-simplify a little, it seems that there are two ways in which a verbal portrait can relate to the conception in the novelist's mind. If he is using a real-life model, or if the portrait is complete in all its details in his imagination, then his task is one of transcription and selection. The former practice is known, of course, but probably isn't common, at least in any crude sense. The latter is virtually an impossibility. Few people have Rhoda Brook's capacity to 'raise a mental image . . . realistic as a photograph' even of close acquaintances. Dickens, the obvious example of a writer who might be thought capable of working in this way, was reluctantly willing to have his mental pictures worked up into actual illustrations by a second imagination. The normal procedure would seem to be that the novelist essaying a long physical description of the Trollopian kind records certain characteristics already present to his own fancy, and tricks them out with a variety of details more or less improvised. Of these, some will fail to 'take', while others will become important aspects of the finished portrait. If Lucy's 'prominent temples', for example, contribute nothing helpful to what is to become Trollope's own effective mental picture of her, then he, and the reader, can forget them. But equally it might happen that in the course of such a description some particular detail – a feature, an expression – takes on life for the author and becomes a controlling element in the portrayal as it eventually emerges. It is as if the Victorian novelist, with plenty of pages at his disposal, can afford to use a few of them for rough sketching – almost for doodling – so that the clear picture is built up through interaction of some of the accumulating notes, as sometimes a Topolski drawing seems to define itself from a tangle of irrelevant pencil-marks. Trollope's paragraphs on Lucy Morris may have served him as a means of developing and intensifying his own conception.

Yet the fact remains that this kind of comprehensive physical portrayal, despite its potentialities, is absent from the work of some of the best nineteenth-century novelists and has virtually disappeared from serious fiction in this century. One explanation, or part-explanation, is that the technique is more suited to some kinds of novel than to others, and may in some instances be quite irrelevant. This is a consideration to which we will return. A more obvious cause seems to lie in the technical limitation of the method. It is, for example, necessarily static. Trollope himself must have felt a little uneasy on that score, because he qualifies his account of Lucy Morris by a subsequent 'apology' :

. . . the poor narrator has been driven to expend his four first
chapters in the mere task of introducing his characters. He regrets
the length of these introductions, and will now begin at once the
action of his story.

In fact this comment is somewhat disingenuous, since the introductions to Lucy and the other characters referred to are not markedly
more detailed than other such passages in his novels. The description
of Lucy is no more elaborate than the portrait of Lady Linlithgow
that succeeds the apology by less than twenty pages. But it is
suggestive that Trollope should feel some sense of awkwardness.

This particular passage was chosen for analysis partly because
Trollope has the difficulty of describing a character whose looks are
in no sense extraordinary. Smollett has a far easier task with the
grotesque Lismahago or Dickens with the monstrous Quilp. Lucy's
face is by no means of 'sterling insignificance', but it is sufficiently
unremarkable to reduce part of Trollope's attempted description to
near-nullity : 'As hair it was very well, but it had no speciality. Her
mouth was somewhat large. . . .' It is as though he were trying to
convey the charming total effect of a fairly conventional set of
features largely by enumerating the latter. There is an essential
weakness in this mode of description that is nicely demonstrated, in
burlesque, by Michael Frayn :

> Some might have called him handsome, but Rick did not think
> of himself as being so. His features were almost classically even,
> but the mouth had a certain humorous twist which made the
> statuesque proportions of the face seem gratefully human. The
> mouth, in fact, was interesting. The regular teeth stood out very
> white amid his deep tan, while the lips were firm but somehow
> sensuous, belying the almost ascetic nose. The eyes were blue –
> like aquamarines nestling among the jeweller's crumpled chamois
> leather as he narrowed his gaze against the hard, almost tangible
> noonday glare. The eyebrows were russet thickets – slightly raised,
> as if surprised and perhaps a little scandalised to find themselves
> sitting on top of a pair of aquamarines. The hair was russet, too
> – cut *en brosse*, and there were fine russet hairs gleaming along
> the forearm raised to ward off the hard, almost tangible noonday
> glare. . . .
>   Rick could feel the roughness of his fingers against his deeply
> sunburnt brow as he gazed. His fingers were long – surprisingly
> long and fine for such a well-built man. The nails were cut
> square, and shone like the mother-of-pearl Rick saw when he was
> skin-diving off the end of the island.

B

The fingers grew from strong, well-formed hands, with russet hair on the back of them, and the hands were attached to the muscular arms by broad, sinewy wrists. There were four fingers and a thumb on each hand. . . .[1]

The extract is from a novel – one of several begun by the aspiring author, Rowe – to be entitled *No Particle Forgot*. The joke can seem painful to anyone who has tried to write a more or less realistic work of fiction. The question of which particles to forget, or omit, seems surprisingly complicated when one is facing a blank page. What is enough? If you fail to mention your hero's nose, will you be leaving a hole in the middle of his face? What is too much? At what point does the descriptive detail begin to be superfluous? Professor Gombrich perhaps provides a clue in *Art and Illusion*, when he remarks : 'We cannot register all the features of a head, and as long as they conform to our expectations they fall silently into the slot of our perceptive apparatus.'[2] The exhaustive description, then, the inventory of features, is false to the psychology of perception. We tend not to notice what is not exceptional. Rowe is certainly wasting his readers' time when he writes of Rick's eyebrows, fingernails and the hair on his wrists. Trollope may well be doing so when he describes Lucy's hair, temples, mouth and feet. Such details may even be counter-productive. Gombrich claims (he is speaking, of course, of painting) that 'the amount of information packed into the picture may hinder the illusion as frequently as it helps it'.[3] Beyond a certain point the 'limitations of the medium' will become obtrusive. It is an impossibility for the painter to record all he sees; any attempt at exhaustiveness will fail and be seen to fail. Just as certainly there can be no such thing as an exhaustive prose-portrait : 'all claims to copy nature must lead to the demand of representing the infinite'.[4] As compared with the painter the prose-writer, for obvious reasons, has much greater difficulty in even approximating to completeness. The major problem lies in the simple fact that print is linear. The greater the amount of detail that is included, the longer the description will be; and the longer the description the less the likelihood that the reader will fuse its successive elements into a single apprehension.

The way out of this dilemma is the same for the novelist as for the portrait-painter. It depends on what Gombrich calls the 'etc. principle' – 'the assumption we tend to make that to see a few members of a series is to see them all'.[5] Thus a painter can copy a head though he cannot hope to reproduce every hair on it. He creates the illusion of reality by depicting enough details to persuade the spectator to fill out the rest of the picture by imaginative extension – by 'projection'. Gombrich suggests that there are two necessary conditions for this response : 'One is that the beholder must be left in no doubt about the way to close the gap; secondly, that he must be given a 'screen', an empty or ill-defined area onto which he can project the expected image.'⁶ The second of these points seems to me a strong argument against the extended prose-portrait. By providing as much information as he does, Trollope leaves no 'screen'. In Gide's phrase he is 'hindering the imagination'. For the fact seems to be that an author cannot effectively describe a face : he can only induce the reader to imagine one; and this process is best initiated by the provision merely of one or two evocative hints. Trollope provides so many details that the reader is discouraged from imaginative participation : there is too little left for him to do.

The question of leaving your audience 'in no doubt about the way to close the gap' is much more problematical for the novelist than for the painter. If it is true that one sees or imagines a face in terms, not of an aggregation of details, but of a prevailing impression merely, then the author must encourage the reader to form such an impression. But the promptings he can offer are limited in kind and scope. The descriptive techniques that are commonest now were all in familiar use by the middle of the last century. The writer could define a face by its shape : round, square, oval, narrow, pointed. He could liken it to the face of a bird, fish, or animal. The horse, the pig, the rat, the ferret, the monkey, the lion and the parrot were among the many creatures used for this purpose. At the risk of over-formality the novelist could follow Fielding's lead and compare his character with a figure in a well-known painting. A more specific and personal effect could be achieved by the vivid depiction of some salient feature. Thus Bagnet, with his whiskers like coconut fibres; Yawler, 'with his nose on one side'; and Fancy Day's father, whose nose has been thrown back in a fight, so that on sunny days people can see 'far into his head'. Certain kinds of face might be expressed solely by the complexion : swarthy, flushed, sallow, mealy. And the novelist who was content to leave everything to the reader could fall back on subjective epithets : evil, handsome, stern, suspicious, timid. There is a logic in this. In inviting his readers to write their own description of Widow Wadman, Sterne is anticipating Gide's theory; but it must be noted that he provides a firm preliminary directive : 'For never did thy eyes behold, or thy concupiscence covet anything in this world, more concupiscible than Widow Wadman.' The blank page he provides is like a blank canvas – but one already bearing the title : 'Portrait of a Concupiscible Widow'. The reader is told, if in the most general terms, what *kind* of attractions to imagine. Sterne's device is, of course, a reminder that any attempt at detailed description is hopelessly undercut by the subjectivity of writer and reader; but it makes a second, less obvious, point. Effectively Sterne is doing no more than the conventional novelist who writes : 'Mary was a very pretty girl.' In either case the reader is invited to 'project'; the simple difference is that Sterne literally provides a 'Screen' for the operation.

In *The Seagull* Chekhov interestingly suggests how the writer can best spark off the process of projection. Trepliov is correcting his own manuscript :

> The description of the moonlit evening is too long and rather precious. Trigorin has worked out his own methods – it comes easily to him. . . . He would just mention the neck of a broken bottle glistening on the dam and the black shadow of a mill-wheel – and there you'd have a moonlit night.[7]

This piece of advice seems to hold good for every sort of description in the novel. But it is particularly apt to descriptions of face or figure, in that these have often to be recalled or re-evoked. When a character reappears in the narrative after a long interval we will need to be reminded what he looks like. The long introductory account will be largely forgotten. As the action of a novel gathers pace it is unlikely to offer scope for further detailed description. What it will permit is the occasional reminder of the hint or two that first stirred the imagination. When a character in fiction seems to have a marked physical presence it is almost always established by this means, by the technique of the Bellman : 'What I tell you three times is true.'

It is a technique that can succeed at a variety of different levels. A mediocre novelist can get you to picture *something*; the power-fully imaginative writer can induce you to see intensely. Again, the visual aspect of the characterisation may be merely a decorative extra, something to 'satisfy the curiosity of the reader'; or it may be vitally relevant to the moral and psychological aspects of the portrayal. It's easy to conceive of a novel which has a great deal of visual life, while lacking any serious significance; but in practice there seem to me to be very few works of this kind. The energy, stamina and consistency of imagination that are necessary to the creation of a strongly visual novel require, almost by definition, the stimulus of some larger purpose.

III

Given the appropriate experimental conditions, which would be extremely difficult to devise, one could test in some detail the extent to which different novelists succeed in providing faces for their characters – faces, that is to say, that the reader pictures and remembers. Here is a very simple exercise of that kind, in the form of a short quiz relating to some of the better-known English novels of the nineteenth century :

1. What colour eyes had :
   (a) Jeanie Deans?
   (b) Emma Woodhouse?
   (c) Heathcliff?
   (d) Becky Sharp?
   (e) Jane Eyre?
   (f) Little Dorrit?
   (g) The Rev. Obadiah Slope?
   (h) Silas Marner?
   (i) Rosamond Vincy?
   (j) Isabel Archer?
2. Which of the following were bearded :
   (a) Edward Murdstone?
   (b) Daniel Deronda?
   (c) Gilbert Osmond?
   (d) Angel Clare?
   (e) Jude Fawley?
3. What colour hair had :
   (a) Fagin?
   (b) Micawber?
   (c) Bathsheba Everdene?
   (d) Maggie Tulliver?
   (e) Little Nell?
   (f) Adam Bede?
   (g) Becky Sharp?
   (h) Milly Theale?
   (i) Rosamond Vincy?
   (j) Marty South?

Answers :
1. (a) grey, (b) hazel, (c) black, (d) green, (e) green, (f) hazel, (g) pale brown, (h) brown, (i) blue, (j) light grey.
2. All but Murdstone.

3. (*a*) red, (*b*) he has none, (*c*) black, (*d*) black, (*e*) light brown, (*f*) jet black, (*g*) sandy, (*h*) red, (*i*) 'of infantile fairness, neither flaxen nor yellow', (*j*) 'a rare and beautiful approximation to chestnut'.

My expectation is that every serious student of nineteenth-century fiction will have known some of these answers, but that virtually no one will have known them all. Since I chose only characters apparently intended to have a significant physical presence, I hope that the quiz might convey some preliminary hints as to what makes for successful (i.e. memorable) and what for unsuccessful portrait-painting. My guess is that 1. (*c*) and (*i*), 3. (*a*), (*b*), (*d*) and (*i*) will have proved particularly easy questions, while 1. (*a*), (*b*), (*f*) and (*j*), 2. (*b*) and (*d*), and 3. (*c*), (*e*) and (*g*) will have proved difficult. I'll explain my reasoning later.

Assembling the questions made me aware of several general points that I had not consciously noted before. For example, there is very little facial hair in the Victorian novel – conspicuously less than in real life. The bearded Dickens produced a long line of beardless heroes. Novelists vary remarkably in their awareness of eyes. Dickens shows little interest in that feature, considering his insistence on physical appearance. But George Eliot tells us the colour of at least nine sets of eyes in *The Mill on the Floss*, including even those of Philip Wakem's deceased mother. Mrs Gaskell describes half a dozen sets in *Wives and Daughters*, though, curiously, Cynthia Kirkpatrick's eyes change from grey in Chapter 19 to blue in Chapter 29. In both novels there is particular emphasis on the colour of the eyes of the heroine – 'black' or 'dark' in Maggie Tulliver's case, grey in the case of Molly Gibson. Hardy is more frugal with such details. Owen Graye, in *Desperate Remedies*, is at one stage required to identify the colour of Mrs Manston's eyes, and finds some difficulty in doing so : '. . . it is not an easy matter to particularize the colour of a stranger's eyes in a merely casual encounter on a path out of doors'. When Hardy does choose to 'particularize' he is often very precise indeed. The eyes of Ethelberta are of 'a disputable stage of colour, between brown and grey'; those of Matilda, in *The Trumpet-Major*, 'would have been called brown, but they were really eel-colour, like many other nice brown eyes . . .'. The fastidiousness of definition is characteristic of Hardy's comments on colour. Ethelberta has 'squirrel-coloured' hair. The hair of Cytherea Graye, in *Desperate Remedies*, 'was of a shining corn yellow in the high lights, deepening to a definite nut brown as each curl wound round into the shade'.

The question of colour is elusive. To decide whether one visualises
in colour when reading a novel can be almost as difficult as deciding
whether one dreams in colour. Again, the response no doubt differs
from individual to individual. For myself I would say that in either
case certain details, at least, have colour – a particular dress may
undoubtedly be red, a particular tree undoubtedly green. And I
could assert confidently that *The Trumpet-Major*, or *Adam Bede*,
or *David Copperfield* is more 'colourful' than *Mansfield Park*, or
The Awkward Age, or *The Way of All Flesh*. *Great Expectations*
and *Oliver Twist* were effectively filmed in black and white; *Far
from the Madding Crowd* surely demanded colour. Indirect
narrative seems to subside naturally towards colourlessness, and so
does any extended account of privation : Gissing is very much a
black-and-white novelist. Historical fiction, because of its emphasis
on costume, tends to be highly coloured.

It might be argued that in the case of Dickens the illustrations
lead us to picture the characters in black and white. The colour
of Little Nell's hair, or of Little Dorrit's eyes can't be caught by
'Phiz', and so is likely to be forgotten. It's surely true, for example,
that the style of Pecksniff's hair ('bolt upright'), which 'Phiz' catches
vividly, is more memorable than its colour ('just grizzled with an
iron-grey'), which he has no means of recording. But the red hair
of Fagin and Heep, and the blue face of Major Bagstock seem to
survive in the recollection naturally enough. In general, Dickens's
illustrators do little to define his heroes and heroines : Pickwick and
Dombey are exceptional cases. Many of the leading characters have
little in the way of a face. The minor characters are much more
fully and vigorously pictured, both by Dickens and by his illustrator,
but facial details tend to be less noticeable than deportment, gesture
and clothes. It is probably easier to remember that Mark Tapley's
neckcloth is red than that his eyes are blue.

Descriptions of colouring often have more to do with temperament than with mere physical appearance. Heathcliff is necessarily
dark; so are Murdstone, Rochester, Henchard, Jaggers. There is an
obvious association between swarthiness and a powerful, even
oppressive, masculinity. The dark ladies of fiction are characteristically passionate, especially if they have a good deal of hair. Maggie
Tulliver, Eustacia Vye, Tattycoram, Alice Marwood and Marian
Halcombe all have notable heads of dark hair. Blonde women tend
to be excessively feminine – frail or flirtatious or both : Rosamond
Vincy, Laura Fairlie, Ginevra Fanshawe. Charlotte Brontë
comments explicitly about the last named : 'Many a time since have
I noticed, in persons of Ginevra Fanshawe's light, careless tempera-

ment, and fair, fragile style of beauty, an entire incapacity to endure. . . .' Facile as such patterns of association may be, they are useful to the novelist : the crude classification can *work*. There may be something novelettish in the physical presentation of Heathcliff, or Rochester, or Fagin the red-haired Jew, or Quilp the hideous dwarf, but perhaps for that very reason each of them comes to life both visually and psychologically.

IV

The guidance that this chapter has offered so far to the novelist who wishes to give his characters faces may be briefly summed up as 'little but often'. The programme isn't as simple as it looks. On occasion even a great novelist may pursue it to very small effect : the character concerned fails to take on an appearance, or the appearance lacks significance, is even, perhaps, a limitation. It may be instructive to look at one or two cases where such an attempt at facial description goes wrong, because these might provide further clues as to how such portraiture can go right. The risk I run, in this very subjective area, is that my examples of relative failure might be seen as successes by another reader. But I hope that any disagreement of that kind might prove illuminating in itself.

George Eliot is an accomplished practitioner of the 'little but often' technique, and she portrays Felix Holt in such terms. When Esther Lyon first meets him she sees that 'The striking points in his face were large clear grey eyes and full lips'. These 'large, grave, candid grey eyes' are mentioned on a number of occasions, but fail to become memorable. They do not relate to anything in Holt's complexion or character : they could as well be brown or blue. His appearance is apparently meant to convey a certain rough-hewn nobility; beyond that it signifies little. As in Eliot's account of Daniel Deronda or Will Ladislaw particularities are obscured by romanticising. The face of a trades-union speaker who addresses a crowd of working men is said to convey 'mere acuteness and rather hard-lipped antagonism'. Then Felix comes forward : 'Even lions and dogs know a distinction between men's glances; and doubtless those Duffield men, in the expectation with which they looked up at Felix, were unconsciously influenced by the grandeur of his full yet firm mouth, and the calm clearness of his grey eyes. . . .' This is all nonsense, of course. George Eliot knows, in fact often preaches, that external appearance is no simple indicator of moral character. Her subjectivity here defeats her technical aims : Holt's face is blurred by sentimental soft focus.

Lucie Manette in *A Tale of Two Cities* is also sentimentalised, but her facelessness is more interesting in that Dickens has clearly made an effort to give her some individuality of appearance. Between the routine golden hair and blue eyes she has 'a forehead with a singular capacity (remembering how young and smooth it was) of lifting and knitting itself into an expression that was not quite one of perplexity, or wonder, or alarm, or merely of a bright fixed attention, though it included all the four expressions . . .'. This is an imaginable and potentially significant characteristic, and Dickens proceeds to allude to it at least half a dozen times in the course of his narrative. But somehow the detail fails to 'take'. This is partly because Dickens is uncertain about the expression : uncertain as to whether it is occasional or habitual, uncertain as to what it conveys. It must go beyond the four possibilities he first mentions, because it is later called Lucie's 'old look of earnestness'. But in her interview with Mr Lorry it becomes 'immovable' and then deepens into a look of 'pain and horror'. It is altogether too versatile an expression to be descriptively useful. In any case the story gives Lucie very little to frown about – very little to do. Her blue eyes and her golden hair are features enough.

A much more surprising failure is Carker in *Dombey and Son.* The problem here is not that the noticeable features of his face will be forgotten, nor that they are inexpressive or unused. Every reader will remember Carker for his smile. His teeth, his lips, his gums are mentioned again and again. The expression is appropriate because, although propitiatory, it shows the dangerous-looking teeth and hints at a snarl. Dickens develops the suggestion of controlled aggressiveness by means of metaphor : Carker is repeatedly likened to a cat. Yet despite this carefulness of technique the face remains oddly difficult to see. Dickens strains too hard, gives us too little, too often. Carker becomes nothing *but* a smile. He is 'the man of teeth'; he passes through the dark rooms of the hotel in Dijon 'like a mouth'. Poor 'Phiz', hopelessly up against it, squeezes some three teeth into a smile one sixteenth of an inch long. The point being made against Carker is too obvious. Either he must look less sinister and predatory than Dickens is constantly implying, or the people around him are hopelessly obtuse. The cat metaphor does little to help the case. A cat's teeth are visible *only* when its snarls, and that snarl looks nothing like a smile. Distractingly, Carker is also compared with a wolf and a shark. As with Felix Holt, the weakness in the portrayal is that the author's strong moral attitude to his character leads to visual over-simplification.

In contrast, I would have thought that Rosamond Vincy and

Maggie Tulliver are two characters who are effectively and economically given visual life. The two portrayals are technically similar.
George Eliot concentrates on a few features only : Maggie's dark
eyes, brown skin and heavy black hair, and Rosamond's blue eyes,
blonde plaits and long neck. Each portrait seems to represent a
recognisable physiognomy or complexion, so that the eyes come to
imply the hair, and vice-versa. Each of the girls is specifically
contrasted with a character of antithetical colouring and temperament. Early in *Middlemarch* Rosamond is shown in the company
of plain, dark, rough-haired Mary Garth, who remarks, on seeing
their twin reflections in a mirror : 'What a brown patch I am by
the side of you, Rosy ! You are the most unbecoming companion.'
Maggie is repeatedly paired with her cousin, Lucy Deane, who is
small, blonde and neat : 'And Maggie always looked twice as dark
as usual when she was by the side of Lucy. . . . It was like the
contrast between a rough, dark, overgrown puppy and a white
kitten.' In either case the physical contrast points up the temperamental contrast. Rosamond, as against Mary Garth, is self-centred,
superficial, narrowly 'feminine'; Maggie, as against the decorous
Lucy, is rebellious, tom-boyish, passionate.

Again, the device may seem a simple one, but, again, it can be
very useful. The novel has always used contrasted pairs of characters
to make moral or psychological points : Thwackum and Square, the
Shandy brothers, the Dashwood sisters. Physical contrast can help to
dramatise the distinctions being made. There need be no association
between particular moral qualities and a particular complexion –
the blonde Rosamond is 'bad', the blonde Lucy 'good' – but the
visual comparison alerts the reader to the moral and temperamental
comparison.

A crucial factor in the depiction of both Rosamond and Maggie
is that their looks are not inert, like those of Felix Holt or Lucie
Manette, but are implicated in the story. Maggie's nonconformity
is suggested by her hair, but is confirmed when she cuts it off. Later
she runs away to the gipsies because she has been made to feel that
her appearance and her wildness are gipsy-like. A turning-point in
Rosamond's career is the moment when she weeps in front of
Lydgate, and the sight of her tears, 'like water on a blue flower', so
melts him that he proposes marriage.

Both portrayals are reinforced with metaphor. Rosamond is associated with flowers, the thick-haired Maggie with ponies and Skye
terriers. In other words the particular physical features that are described are made to contribute also to an impressionistic account of the
character. Dickens, despite the over-simplification with Carker, is an

adept at this technique. The blue-faced dilating Major Bagstock is in any case a wonderfully visual creation; but Dickens frequently makes a double point by describing his appearance through metaphors drawn from the rich foodstuffs that have helped to produce it : 'his complexion like a Stilton cheese, and his eyes like a prawn's . . .'.

The 'little but often' slogan, then, offers inadequate help to the would-be novelist. To be truly memorable the features that are emphasised should contribute to several systems of relationship. They should relate to each other, and to the temperament of the character concerned; they may relate to the features of other characters, to the action of the story, to patterns of metaphor. A powerful physical portrait is invariably sustained by a sub-structure of cross-reference, because the novelist's response to faces implies, and is likely to be involved with, his response to life in general. The next section of this chapter will illustrate that view at some length; but here, first, is a more limited example of the complex suggestiveness that can inform the physical depiction of a major character. It provides I hope, an instructive comparison with Dickens's account of Carker.

The reader of *Anna Karenin* is only gradually made aware of Vronsky's most noticeable facial feature :

. . . every time he thought of the helmet he would burst into roars of hearty laughter, showing his strong, even teeth.

'What?' said Vronsky angrily, making a grimace of disgust and showing his even teeth.

He laughed cheerfully, showing his regular teeth. . . .

. . . he added, smiling and showing his fine, white teeth.

. . . raising his head with a smile that showed his fine teeth.

. . . said Vronsky, displaying his fine white teeth in a friendly smile.

. . . with a serene smile that showed his even teeth. . . .

. . . showing his strong white teeth in a smile.[8]

The list is by no means exhaustive, but I have made it reasonably long in order to suggest how sustained the reference is. Tolstoy's device is in a small way dramatic, in that Vronsky's teeth are on display only when he smiles or grimaces, when he is actively responding to a situation, expressing a mood. The visual reminder is incorporated into the action. He shows his teeth often, because

he often smiles. From the first he is characterised as a friendly
good-humoured man, with considerable personal charm. The smile
is part of that charm – a charm that the reader is likely to feel and
to respond to. But the strong teeth also come to suggest another
side of Vronsky's nature. In conjunction with his heavy jaws, deep
chest, strong legs and general athleticism they imply the vigorous
masculinity that can make him on occasion not merely competitive
but aggressive and harsh, capable of kicking his fallen mare in the
stomach. The references to his teeth become hinted reminders of
potential brutality. Anna is to see him 'hard as a flint', 'cruel' and
'menacing'. After their final interview, which is to lead directly to
Anna's suicide, he jumps up, intending to run after her : 'but on
second thoughts he sat down again, firmly setting his teeth and
frowning'. His masculine hardness prevails, and Anna is destroyed.

The fine teeth and the touch of menace in the smile may recall
Carker, but the similarity is only superficial. Physically Carker is
notable only for his teeth, and Dickens mentions them forty or fifty
times. Vronsky's appearance and physique are established in detail :
the balding head, the red neck, the moustaches, the hairy chest –
even his weight : eleven and a half stone. Carker's smile expresses
only flattery, gloating, malignity; Vronsky's is cheerful and open,
and can suggest a variety of moods. The point of comparing the
two portrayals is not to labour differences of quality or kind –
obviously Dickens deliberately limits and stylises his characterisation
of Carker – but to highlight the enormous potentiality of the device
used so restrictedly in *Dombey and Son*. For there is a sense in which
Vronsky's character, like Carker's, is displayed in his teeth. On his
last appearance he is leaving for a probably unjust war, hoping to
rid himself of a life that has become 'loathsome' to him : '. . . as a
weapon I may be of some use. But as a man I'm a wreck.' He gets
out these words only with difficulty because of 'the incessant gnaw-
ing ache in his tooth', 'the agonizing pain in the big tooth, which
filled his mouth with saliva'. Only the greater pain of his remorse
over Anna can make him forget the toothache. His teeth are in the
same plight as himself, and similarly suggest masculine power in
decay. The incidental descriptive references have been caught up,
and their significance consummated.

V

November 11. Met Lady Cynthia Graham. In appearance she is
something like my idea of Tess, though I did not know her when
the novel was written.[9]

It is interesting to learn that Hardy's 'idea' of his heroine was so specific that he could be reminded of her by a real person. But, then, the physical portrayal of Tess is extraordinarily full and sustained. The descriptive passages are too numerous and varied to be easily summarised. Mrs Clare, who has never met Tess, offers the nearest thing to a thumbnail sketch, on the basis of her son's account :

> 'I can see her quite distinctly. You said the other day that she was fine in figure; roundly built; had deep red lips like Cupid's bow; dark eyelashes and brows, an immense rope of hair like a ship's cable; and large eyes violety-bluey-blackish.'

Each of these details is established through repeated references, some incidental, some extended. The 'mobile peony mouth' is described with particular care on Tess's first appearance :

> The pouted-up deep red mouth . . . had hardly as yet settled into its definite shape, and her lower lip had a way of thrusting the middle of her top one upward, when they closed together after a word.

Tess's 'cable of dark-brown hair', sometimes coiled up and sometimes hanging straight down her back, is mentioned again and again. So are the 'deep dark eyes' :

> . . . large tender eyes, neither black nor blue nor gray nor violet; rather all those shades together, and a hundred others, which could be seen if one looked into their irises – shade beyond shade – tint beyond tint – around pupils that had no bottom. . . .

Elsewhere Hardy refers to 'the ever-varying pupils, with their radiating fibrils of blue, and black, and gray, and violet . . .'. Not every reader will knowingly have seen eyes of this type. Those who have will recognise the description at once, and will respond to its precision.

Hardy defines Tess's face, then, in terms of the hair, the eyes and the mouth – each of these features being strongly marked and repeatedly mentioned. It is a vivid sketch. But much of the power of the presentation lies in the author's awareness of development and change in his heroine's appearance. He provides a glimpse of her as a school-girl, when her hair was 'earth-coloured' and hung 'like pot-hooks'. He shows how it seems to double in quantity when it has just been washed, or how it falls below her bonnet in the rain and becomes as clammy as seaweed. As Tess changes from girl to woman, following the death of her baby, 'Her eyes grew larger and more eloquent'. Angel sees her eyelids heavy with sleep, or drooping with grief. In Tess's terror, after her marriage-night story has alienated him, 'her mouth had almost the aspect of a round little hole'. A little later 'the usually ripe red mouth was almost as pale as her cheek'. Hardy persuades us that her looks can vary appreciably with her situation, with the weather, even with the time of day. He remarks, when describing her journey to Talbothays :

> Her face had latterly changed with changing states of mind, continually fluctuating between beauty and ordinariness, according as the thoughts were gay or grave. One day she was pink and flawless; another pale and tragical.

At daybreak she looks to Angel Clare like a goddess, 'a visionary essence of woman' :

> Then it would grow lighter, and her features would become simply feminine; they had changed from those of a divinity who could confer bliss to those of a being who craved it.

Such passages contribute to a pattern of allusions that keeps the reader constantly aware of the beauty, the resilience, the vulnerability of Tess's physical form – the form that decides her fortunes. Lying at night in a wood, among dying pheasants, she 'put her hand to her brow, and felt its curve, and the edges of her eye-sockets perceptible under the soft skin, and thought as she did so that a time would come when that bone would be bare'. The sense of mortality comes home to us because we know Tess's body intimately. We see her trembling, perspiring, sleeping, bleeding, weeping. Looking at her through Angel's eyes, the eyes of a lover, we become sensuously aware of her. When she yawns he sees 'the red interior of her mouth as if it had been a snake's'. When he embraces her the slanting sun shines 'upon her inclining face, upon the blue veins of her temple, upon her naked arm, and her neck, and into the depths of her hair'. Angel touches her cheek with a finger, and *feels* her blush rising. When he kisses 'the inside vein of her soft arm' he finds her 'such a sheaf of susceptibilities that her pulse was accelerated by the touch, her blood driven to her finger-ends, and the cool arms flushed hot'.

Altogether Tess's physical existence, as a being of skin and blood and bone and nerves, is realised as fully as her spiritual or psychological existence. Tess is a unique individual, 'a woman living her precious life – a life which, to herself who endured or enjoyed it, possessed as great a dimension as the life of the mightiest to himself'. But as a physical organism she is part of the natural order, responsive to the same needs and appetites as beasts and birds and even plants. She is linked with Nature in scores of incidental images :

. . . her large eyes staring at him like those of a wild animal.

. . . his lips touching cheeks that were damp and smoothly chill as the skin of the mushrooms in the fields around.

. . . some spirit within her rose automatically as the sap in the twigs.

. . . she was warm as a sunned cat.

. . . like a bird caught in a clap-net. . . .

. . . she was surcharged with emotion, and winced like a wounded animal.

Tess's lips being parted like a half-opened flower near his cheek.

This list (which could be greatly extended) is a clumsy device, but it seemed the only way of suggesting the pervasiveness of the process of assimilation that is so vital to Hardy's portrayal of Tess. Sometimes he makes his point explicitly. Tess is a field-woman, and :

. . . a field-woman is a portion of the field; she has somehow lost her own margin, imbibed the essence of her surrounding, and assimilated herself with it.

Thus Tess walks on; a figure which is part of the landscape; a field-woman pure and simple, in winter guise. . . .

Where Tess is associated with the more obviously attractive aspects of Nature the effect is flattering; she seems wholesome, vital, desirable : '. . . often had he said gaily that her mouth and breath tasted of the butter and eggs and milk and honey on which she mainly lived . . . '. But Hardy's larger purpose is to set Tess's short life firmly in the context of Nature, and by doing so to pose certain important questions. Is Man primarily an animal or a spiritual being? Are Tess's sufferings, are human sufferings in general, simply aspects of the conflicts and wastage within Nature? How far can Man control or modify his fate?

From one point of view Tess's case is an exceptional one. She is particularly beautiful. She is descended from an 'ancient and knightly family'. Her National School education takes her to an intellectual level beyond the reach of her parents. Exceptionally enough she commits murder and is hanged for it. But Hardy also makes Tess a typical figure. She is first seen as one of a troop of women and girls, 'not handsomer than some others, possibly . . .'. She is one of seven children, two others having died. As a school-girl she 'used to be seen about the village as one of three – all nearly of the same year – walking home from school side by side; Tess the middle one . . .'. At Talbothays she is frequently in the company of her fellow-milkmaids, Retty, Marian and Izz, and the four of them are united in their love for Angel Clare: 'The differences which distinguished them as individuals were abstracted by this passion, and each was but portion of one organism called sex.' Tess is not categorically more interesting than the others. All are 'blooming young women'. Retty Priddle, like herself, is descended from an ancient landed family. All four are made wretched by their love for Angel. Izz almost goes to Brazil with him in Tess's place; perhaps, like Tess, she is betrayed by her own honesty. Marian takes to drink. Retty attempts suicide, and later goes into a decline: 'Nobody will ever fall in love wi' her any more.' It is because Hardy has generalised Tess's experiences and sufferings in these ways that Clare's final departure with 'Liza-Lu – 'a spiritualized image of Tess, slighter than she, but with the same beautiful eyes' – seems more than an empty consolatory gesture to the reader.

The obvious point that Hardy is making is a democratic one – each of these girls is a unique being, with a story worth telling. It need not be an absurd undertaking to write a novel entitled *Retty of the Paridelles.* Angel Clare's work at Talbothays destroys his notion of a 'typical and unvarying Hodge': 'He had been disinte-grated into a number of varied fellow-creatures – beings of many minds, beings infinite in difference; some happy, many serene, a few depressed, one here and there bright even to genius, some stupid, others wanton, others austere. . . .' Tess herself hates the idea of being 'one of a long row only': 'The best is not to remember that your nature and your past doings have been just like thousands' and thousands', and that your coming life and doings 'll be like thousands' and thousands'.' Yet Hardy often reduces individuality towards vanishing-point. It is not merely that the milkmaids have so much in common; the entire staff of Talbothays can seem to blend into a featureless group, as when they are scouring a field for garlic: 'Differing one from another in natures and moods so greatly as they did, they yet formed, bending, a curiously uniform row –

automatic, noiseless; and an alien observer passing down the neigh-
bouring lane might well have been excused for massing them as
"Hodge".' There are even fundamental affinities between man and
animals, man and plants. In hot July : 'the atmosphere of the flat
vale hung heavy as an opiate over the dairy-folk, the cows, and the
trees'. The farmworkers doze in the afternoons, when 'the animals,
the very bees and butterflies' are drowsy. The regenerative impulse,
the 'appetite for joy' that restores Tess after the loss of her baby,
'pervades all life', 'pervades all creation'. Her revival is part of the
annual revival of nature. In her misfortunes she is no unluckier
than Prince, or the wounded pheasants, or the rabbits, hares, snakes,
rats and mice that are trapped by the reapers.

The assimilative images that describe Tess are an expression of
this sense of a oneness in nature. Hardy has, in general, a unifying
habit of metaphor. He speaks of 'a monstrous pumpkin-like moon'.
The milkmaids cling to a roadside bank 'like pigeons on a roof-
slope'. The teats of some of the cows are 'as hard as carrots'.
Throughout the Talbothays section the writing is powerfully
synaesthetic, merging different kinds of experience indistinguishably
together. The first words that the sleepy Tess hears concerning
Angel Clare 'seemed to be generated by the darkness in which they
floated'. They come to her 'along with the smell of the cheeses in
the adjoining cheese-loft, and the measured dripping of the whey
from the wrings downstairs'. Later Clare is to woo her 'in under-
tones like that of the purling milk'. When she listens to him playing
the harp its harmonies 'passed like breezes through her. . . . The
floating pollen seemed to be his notes made visible . . . the rank-
smelling weed-flowers glowed as if they would not close for intentness,
and the waves of colour mixed with the waves of sound.' The
responses of the lovers to one another are inextricably mingled with
their responses to their surroundings, to the season, to the weather.
Tess of the d'Urbervilles makes it easy to understand why Proust
should have been an admirer of Hardy.

For Angel Clare, the idealist, Tess comes to epitomise all the
varied beauty of a way of life that has stirred his senses and
redeemed him from 'chronic melancholy'. He reciprocates the love
of all the milkmaids in his love for her. It is because he sees Tess in
this light – 'no longer the milkmaid, but a visionary essence of
woman' – that he cannot come to terms with her individuality.
Undergraduate readers commonly find Angel a pompous bore, and
the reaction is understandable. Confronted with the abundance of
Tess he can address her as Artemis and Demeter, can exclaim to
himself : 'What a fresh and virginal daughter of Nature that milk-

maid is!' Having exalted her in this way, quite contrary to her own wishes, he later blames and deserts her for having deceived him : 'You were one person; now you are another.' But simply to condemn Angel for sentimentality or obtuseness, even though he blames himself, is to misconstrue the novel. Angel proclaims – it is the main reason for the doleful weightiness of his diction – the eternal human tendency to compound love, sexual desire and a response to the beauties of nature. Far from belittling or satirising that tendency Hardy's novel celebrates it. Of course there is an ironic contrast between Angel's idealising and Tess's corporeality. Hardy makes the point particularly pleasantly when Clare is studying her lips : '. . . as they again confronted him, clothed with colour and life, they sent an *aura* over his flesh, a breeze through his nerves, which wellnigh produced a qualm; and actually produced, by some mysterious physiological process, a prosaic sneeze'. But the novel shows again and again that life cannot – not merely should not, but cannot – be reduced to the physical. During her unhappy pregnancy Tess wanders at twilight :

> At times her whimsical fancy would intensify natural processes around her till they seemed a part of her own story. Rather they became a part of it; for the world is only a psychological phenomenon, and what they seemed they were.

This verges on over-statement : presumably Flintcomb-Ash, for example, would look dreary to anyone's eyes. But it is surely the mood of Tess and Angel, rather than the season, that transforms Talbothays for them when they return after their marriage : 'The gold of the summer picture was now gray, the colours mean, the rich soil mud, and the river cold.' Even at the height of summer nature can reflect Tess's unhappiness : 'The evening sun was now ugly to her, like a great inflamed wound in the sky.' Hardy believes, with Wordsworth, that human beings inevitably create as they perceive. Like Angel he is ready to see Tess as a 'divinity' when she is transfigured by certain lights or moods or situations. Our disposition to impose meanings upon our sensual impressions or physical appetites is as real as those impressions or appetites themselves. Certainly Angel's idealisation of Tess forces a false personality upon her; but in Hardy's view we are all, in a sense, split personalities – thinking animals. If Angel misreads his wife's situation she, too, misreads it. Indeed, there can be no 'situation' independent of human misreadings : what it seems it is.

The extreme duality of Hardy's vision is brilliantly expressed through the physical presentation of Tess. The body that he so lavishly, so sensually describes she can leave behind by listening to music or gazing at a star. When Angel meets Tess in Sandbourne he sees that she 'had spiritually ceased to recognize the body before him as hers – allowing it to drift, like a corpse upon the current, in a direction dissociated from its living will'. The essential Tess need not be, and finally is not, imprisoned by the flesh that often seems to define both her being and her destiny. Hardy's portrait of her dramatises ideas that would have little force if reduced to direct authorial comment. The contradiction it involves takes on profound meaning because it is developed and explored through scores of interconnected descriptive details.

VI

I hope that this chapter will have shown, among other things, how easily passages of description may fail to produce the intended effect, whether through redundancy, triviality or inconsistency. A converse possibility naturally presents itself. Is a negative failure conceivable? Could absence of description damage or limit a novel?

One or two of my earlier arguments might seem to imply that this is unlikely. It was suggested that Hardy's richly physical presentation of Tess derived from his views about life in general. Perhaps a quite different set of views could give rise to a mode of fiction that scarcely dealt in description at all. It might be held, for example, that Jane Austen quite properly refuses to depict faces because she is siding with Sense against Sensibility: morals and manners are more important to her than physical appearance. Her preliminary account of Henry Crawford suggests that the case could be broadened still further :

. . . when they first saw him, he was absolutely plain, black and plain; but still he was the gentleman, with a pleasing address. The second meeting proved him not so very plain; he was plain, to be sure, but then he had so much countenance, and his teeth were so good, and he was so well made, that one soon forgot he was plain; and after a third interview, after dining in company with him at the parsonage, he was no longer to be called so by any body. He was, in fact, the most agreeable young man the sisters had ever known, and they were equally delighted with him.

Jane Austen's moral views need not enter the matter. She is describing an environment within which masculine good looks, beyond a certain basic requirement, count for much less than wit and charm. Why should she delineate features that the Bertram sisters in effect don't see? Even her more trifling female characters find romantic attraction chiefly in an agreeable manner, 'a pleasing address'; and these qualities are best displayed through dialogue.

But the admirer of Jane Austen could equally take a very different line. I have been arguing that the novelist can usually afford to emphasise only a few physical features of a character, and that these take on significance chiefly through a relationship with other factors – temperament, attitudes, actions, speech-style. Might not such factors in themselves be sufficient to induce the reader to hypothesise an appropriate face? Common experience suggests that this must happen at least in some cases. It seems perfectly reasonable to say of a television serialisation of *Pride and Prejudice*, for instance, that Elizabeth looks wrong or that Mr Bennet looks right. There would probably even be a measure of general agreement on certain points : Mr Bennet must be lean rather than fat; Elizabeth must be dark rather than fair. The manner of these characters implies their appearance, at least in general terms. Elizabeth presumably looks pretty and spirited; Mr Bennet presumably looks sardonic. Would Jane Austen have been adding anything significant if she had described Mr Bennet as having, say, 'a thin, dark, sardonic face with sharp grey eyes'?

Until far into the nineteenth century it remained a tradition that the hero or heroine could be left undescribed, or could be described in idealised language. The reader was tacitly invited to picture for himself a beautiful girl or a handsome young man. This was the Widow Wadman technique. Why should not such an epithet as 'plain', 'sardonic', 'humorous', 'merry', 'bureaucratic' be left, similarly, to the subjectivity of the reader? One could surely imagine, as indeed one could attempt to draw, a sardonic face. Is much to be gained by an attempt to be visually more specific?

A preliminary answer to such questions is that the reader looks for the degree of visual precision that the story requires and that the manner of narration encourages him to expect. The second of these points is the less problematical. Little Dorrit's hazel eyes are easily, and in a sense rightly, forgotten, because it is in her nature to be unnoticeable. Her first appearance in the novel is a curious retrospective affair. Clennam belatedly recalls that a girl has been present during his reunion with his mother : 'It was a girl, surely . . . almost hidden in the dark corner?' The reader has not been allowed to spot her at all. But this negative introduction is true to her character, and the subsequent lack of description seems apt, even necessary. The case is very different, however, with Agnes Wickfield. Ostensibly David Copperfield pictures her time and again; but the adjectives are always abstract ones : 'bright', 'pleasant', 'placid', 'sweet', 'calm', 'gentle', 'quiet', 'radiant', 'tender', 'cheerful', 'modest', 'thoughtful', 'cordial', 'serene'. There is far too much of all this. With the best will in the world such a variety of adjectives can't well be fused into a visual impression. In any case the reader has become accustomed to descriptions a good deal more specific. The portrait of Uriah Heep is elaborately and unappetisingly physical. He might well pose, as he is obviously intended to, a very nasty sexual threat – but scarcely to Agnes. He could as well attempt to molest a rainbow. Dora Spenlow has her limitations, but she is physically *there*, small and girlish, with blue eyes and thick curls. In contrast Agnes is physically so null that David's growth to maturity seems to involve exchanging a wife with no mind for a wife with no body. Dickens has encouraged us to expect particularised description. Where he fails to supply it he leaves a hole or a smudge in the reader's imaginative response to his novel.

But the problem has an interesting counterpart. In a novel that deals very little in physical detail any such information that is included can seem disproportionately emphatic. The unfortunate Mrs Clay, in *Persuasion*, has freckles and a 'projecting tooth'. In the context Jane Austen creates these minor deficiencies loom large. A well-bred woman, such as Lady Russell, has for descriptive purposes neither skin nor teeth. The freckles must be very marked, the projecting tooth very prominent, if they demand recording. Presumably Mrs Clay was intended to appear quite attractive, if in a rather coarse style. She emerges as obtrusively plain, unimaginable either as a threat to Sir Walter or as a mistress for Mr Elliot.

More is involved here than a minor miscalculation. Mrs Clay cannot well be left undescribed because her appearance is relevant to her role in the novel. Normally Jane Austen's characters meet and inter-act in secure social situations where physical attractiveness is of relatively minor significance, and so can be ignored or taken for granted by writer and reader. But when one of them is induced to violate the proprieties for reasons of sexual desire the case is changed. The onus is on the author to make the development plausible. If Mrs Clay is a positive failure, Lydia Bennet is a negative one. Surely it is necessary to *Pride and Prejudice* that Lydia should be strikingly pretty? On no other assumption could Wickham's elopement with her be explained, since her conversation is unrelievedly vulgar and stupid. But she has no physical presence : Jane Austen credits her with nothing but 'youth and a tolerable person'. The episode, as it stands, is incredible, and the characterisation of Wickham is needlessly impaired.

Bleak House offers a rather different example of an author failing to provide the visual detail that his story demands. As John Carey remarks : 'Esther Summerson's smallpox means nothing to us because, so far as we are concerned, she has no face.'[10] It is because a particular situation requires us to look hard at Esther's face that we notice its absence. There is a similar awkwardness in *Mansfield Park*, when Jane Austen hurriedly beautifies Fanny Price in order to make it feasible for Henry Crawford to be attracted by her. To be told that Fanny's looks have improved is to be made aware that she had had no looks.

The unquestioned, unthreatened beauty of the traditional heroine poses no such problems, but by the same token it is less interesting. The Widow Wadman technique can only work when the character concerned is granted immunity from many of the painful or embarrassing contingencies of real life. The novelist who idealises the appearance of his hero and heroine, but describes his minor characters realistically, builds a class-barrier into his fiction. The early work of Dickens is limited in just this way. Cruikshank's illustrations are faithful to the text of *Oliver Twist* in making Oliver appear to belong to a different species from Nancy or the Artful Dodger. There is a comparable stylistic gulf between Little Nell and Kit Nubbles, Mary Graham and Sarah Gamp. Esther's passing disfigurement, Little Dorrit's physical insignificance are attempts to bridge that gap, to do away with stylistic privilege. A century earlier, for similar reasons, Fielding broke Amelia's nose. The novelist who is willing to expose his major characters in this way enormously increases the potential range of his work, but runs a number of risks. *Amelia* was a stylistically uncertain book, and its heroine was derided for her noselessness.

In a successful novel the story and the way in which that story is told will be finely adjusted as to scope and emphasis. The narration will automatically exclude material extrinsic to the action. Jane Austen and Henry James can usually keep physical description to a minimum because their fiction is so largely concerned with conversation and social conduct. In Hardy and Eliot, where sensual responsiveness is intrinsic to action and narration, there are far more faces and bodies. The difficulty in this mode is that of maintaining consistency. The more physical information the reader is given, the more he expects. If Esther's face is 'very much changed' by her illness, what did it look like before? If Uriah Heep's hair is red, what colour is Agnes's? If Amelia's 'lovely nose' is 'beat all to pieces', how does the surgeon put it together again? The realist writer must either answer such questions or find a technique for averting them.

When James and Austen do oblige themselves to cope with the physical world they can both seem uneasy. Milly Theale's appearance is as unsatisfactory as her illness. But their reluctance to describe results only occasionally in specific gaps or 'faults'. The obvious sacrifice that they knowingly make is the neglect of many of the emotions and appetites and experiences of actual life. But perhaps even in the stories that they do choose to tell there is a limitation, a thinness. The Widow Wadman technique can only achieve so much. The great nineteenth-century novelists who tried hard to be specific about the appearance of their characters were concerned with two vital effects : definition and intensity. It might have been feasible for George Eliot to describe Lucy Deane merely as 'pretty'; But Maggie Tulliver's looks could never have been categorised so simply. And Maggie, like Tess, becomes what she becomes partly because her looks are of an unusual kind. The reader must see these characters, and see them clearly, if he is to understand them. It seems to me that such a response involves not merely a different, but an ampler, kind of knowledge. Elinor Dashwood or Kate Croy may take on sufficient visual life for the roles assigned to them, but they certainly have none to spare. Physically insubstantial and imperceptive, they lack a vital dimension. We 'believe in' them, of course, but we believe in Tess Durbeyfield or Maggie Tulliver more variously, more profoundly, because they have a sensual, as well as a moral and intellectual, existence.

Chapter 3

Gesture

It is an incident for a woman to stand up with her hand resting on a table and look out at you in a certain way; or if it be not an incident I think it will be hard to say what it is. If you say you don't see it (character in *that* – *allons donc*!), this is exactly what the artist who has reason of his own for thinking he *does* see it undertakes to show you.

Henry James, *The Art of Fiction*

They occupied the two chairs, and Mr Fips took the office stool, from the stuffing whereof he drew forth a piece of horse-hair of immense length, which he put into his mouth with a great appearance of appetite.

Charles Dickens, *Martin Chuzzlewit*

His attentive face relaxed a little. But I saw one of his feet, softly, quietly, incessantly beating on the carpet under the table, and I felt that he was secretly as anxious as ever.

Wilkie Collins, *Woman in White*

The Squire was put out; and when he was put out he had a trick of placing his hands on his knees and whistling softly to himself.

Elizabeth Gaskell, *Wives and Daughters*

. . . leaving Lush time to mingle some admiration of her graceful back with that half-amused sense of her spirit and impertinence, which he expressed by raising his eyebrows and just thrusting his tongue between his teeth.

George Eliot, *Daniel Deronda*

The friend of the family was in that stage of the tender passion which bound him to regard everybody else as the foe of the family. He put the round head of his cane in his mouth, like a stopper, when he sat down. As if he felt himself full to the throat with affronting sentiments.

Charles Dickens, *Our Mutual Friend*

Standing before her with his hands behind him and his legs a little apart, he swayed slightly to and fro, inclined towards her as if rising on his toes. It had an effect of conscientious deliberation.

Henry James, *The Wings of the Dove*

'Where do you suppose, now:' the doctor closed one eye, as he leaned back smilingly in his chair, and formed a triangle with his hands, of which his two thumbs composed the base: 'where do you suppose Mr Crimple's stomach is?'

Charles Dickens, *Martin Chuzzlewit*

'It's Mrs Scales to the life – I can see that,' said Lily.

'Yes,' said Constance. 'Whenever there was a wind she always stood like that, and took long deep breaths of it.'

This recollection of one of Sophia's habits recalled the whole woman to Constance's memory, and drew a picture of her character for the girl who had scarcely known her.

Arnold Bennett, *The Old Wives' Tale*

'But still, look is a good deal,' observed grandfather William absently, moving and balancing his head till the tip of grandfather James's nose was exactly in a right line with William's eye and the mouth of a miniature cavern he was discerning in the fire.

Thomas Hardy, *Under the Greenwood Tree*

'No doubt she will,' said the miller; 'for I have never known thee wanting in sense in a jineral way.' He turned his cup round on its axis till the handle had travelled a complete circle. 'How long did you say in your letter that you had known her?'

Thomas Hardy, *The Trumpet-Major*

He was a secret-looking man whom I had never seen before. His head was all on one side, and one of his eyes was half shut up, as if he were taking aim at something with an invisible gun. He had a pipe in his mouth, and he took it out, and, after slowly blowing all his smoke away and looking hard at me all the time, nodded.

Charles Dickens, *Great Expectations*

'It's a fine morning, honest Thady, says she; good bye to ye' – and into the carriage she stept, without a word more, good or bad, or even half-a-crown; but I made my bow, and stood to see her safe out of sight for the sake of the family.

Maria Edgeworth, *Castle Rackrent*

While he followed the house-servant along the passage, and through the kitchen, stepping cautiously on every dark mark in the pattern of the oil-cloth, in order to conceal his dirty footprints, Margaret ran upstairs.

Elizabeth Gaskell, *North and South*

Messrs Codlin and Short, after looking at each other with considerable doubt and indecision, at length sat down – each on the extreme edge of the chair pointed out to him – and held their hats very tight. . . .

Charles Dickens, *Old Curiosity Shop*

No sir, I do not bite my thumb at you sir, but I bite my thumb sir.

William Shakespeare, *Romeo and Juliet*

Moving on beside him, she slipped her hand softly within his arm; but Jasper did not put the arm into position to support hers, and her hand fell again, dropped suddenly.

George Gissing, *New Grub Street*

As a matter of course, Messrs Pyke and Pluck stared at the individual whom Sir Mulberry Hawk stared at; so the poor Colonel, to hide his confusion, was reduced to the necessity of holding his port before his right eye and affecting to scrutinise its colour with the most lively interest.

Charles Dickens, *Nicholas Nickleby*

As he said this, Ralph clenched his left wrist tightly with his right hand, and inclining his head a little on one side and dropping his chin upon his breast, looked at him whom he addressed with a frowning, sullen face: the very picture of a man whom nothing could move or soften.

Charles Dickens, *Nicholas Nickleby*

Deans raised the Bible with his left hand, so as partly to screen his face, and putting back his right as far as he could, held it towards Butler in that position, at the same time turning his body from him, as if to prevent his seeing the working of his countenance.

Sir Walter Scott, *Heart of Midlothian*

The whole party followed, with the exception of Scythrop, who threw himself into his arm-chair, crossed his left foot over his right knee, placed the hollow of his left hand on the interior ancle of his left leg, rested his right elbow on the elbow of the chair, placed the ball of his right thumb against his right temple,

curved the forefinger along the upper part of his forehead, rested
the point of the middle finger on the bridge of his nose, and the
points of the two others on the lower part of the palm, fixed his
eyes intently on the veins in the back of his left hand, and sat in
this position like the immoveable Theseus. . . . We hope the
admirers of the *minutiae* in poetry and romance will appreciate
this accurate description of a pensive attitude.

Thomas Love Peacock, *Nightmare Abbey*

She sat in the attitude which denotes unflagging, intense concentrated thought – as if she were cast in bronze. Her feet were
together, her body bent a little forward, and quite unsupported by
the back of the chair; her hands on her knees, her eyes fixed
intently on the corner of a footstool.

At last she moved and tapped her fingers upon the table at her
side. Her pent-up ideas had finally found some channel to
advance in. Motions became more and more frequent as she
laboured to carry further and further the problem which occupied
her brain. She sat back and drew a long breath: she sat sideways
and leant her forehead upon her hand. Later still she arose,
walked up and down the room – at first abstractedly, with her
features as firmly set as ever; but by degrees her brow relaxed,
her footsteps became lighter and more leisurely; her head rose
gracefully and was no longer bowed. She preened herself like a
swan after exertion.

Thomas Hardy, *Desperate Remedies*

The girl beat her hands upon her knees, and her feet upon the
ground; and, suddenly stopping, drew her shawl close round her:
and shivered with cold.

Charles Dickens, *Oliver Twist*

. . . and when one of them told the others about it, they put their
hands in their pockets, and quite doubled themselves up with
laughter, and went stamping about the pavement of the hall.

Charles Dickens, *Bleak House*

Accordingly, he took the paper and lowered his spectacles,
measured the space at his command, reached his pen and
examined it, dipped it in the ink and examined it again, then
pushed the paper a little way from him, lifted up his spectacles
again, showed a deepened depression in the outer angle of his
bushy eyebrows, which gave his face a peculiar mildness (pardon
these details for once – you would have learned to love them if
you had known Caleb Garth). . . .

George Eliot, *Middlemarch*

As Arthur came over the stile and down to the water's edge, the lounger glanced at him for a moment, and then resumed his occupation of idly tossing stones into the water with his foot. There was something in his way of spurning them out of their places with his heel, and getting them into the required position, that Clennam thought had an air of cruelty in it. Most of us have more or less frequently derived a similar impression, from a man's manner of doing some very little thing: plucking a flower, clearing away an obstacle, or even destroying an insentient object.

Charles Dickens, *Little Dorrit*

Here a beautiful practice might be cited, now much in abeyance: the hat-lifting rule. When, according to traditional, official etiquette, a gentleman was thanked by a strange lady for his holding the door open, or offering her a seat in a public conveyance, or picking up a dropped parcel and proffering it to her, or saving her from a runaway horse, he bowed slightly and raised his hat, all the while specifically not returning her gaze. That motion allowed him to imply that the act was but a single expression of the worthiness of the recipient's self based upon her gender attributes, that he acknowledges the obligation of orienting himself to such qualities and to the passing predicaments of their possessor, and that the exchange has been brought to a close.

Erving Goffman, *Relations in Public*

The yeomen, farmers, dairymen, and townsfolk, who came to transact business in these ancient streets, spoke in other ways than by articulation. Not to hear the words of your interlocutor in metropolitan centres is to know nothing of his meaning. Here the face, the arms, the hat, the stick, the body throughout spoke equally with the tongue. To express satisfaction the Casterbridge market-man added to his utterance a broadening of the cheeks, a crevicing of the eyes, a throwing back of the shoulders, which was intelligible from the other end of the street. If he wondered . . . you knew it from perceiving the inside of his crimson mouth, and a target-like circling of his eyes. Deliberation caused sundry attacks on the moss of adjoining walls with the end of his stick, a change of his hat from the horizontal to the less so; a sense of tediousness announced itself in a lowering of the person by spreading the knees to a lozenge-shaped aperture and contorting the arms.

Thomas Hardy, *The Mayor of Casterbridge*

There is not a secret so aiding to the progress of sociality, as to get master of this *short hand*, and be quick in rendering the several turns of looks and limbs, with all their inflections and delineations, into plain words. For my own part, by long habitude, I do it so mechanically, that when I walk the streets of London, I go translating all the way; and have more than once stood behind in the circle, where not three words have been said, and have brought off twenty different dialogues with me, which I could have fairly wrote down and sworn to.

Laurence Sterne, *A Sentimental Journey*

Almost in despair I nodded, and added to my smile such gestures indicative of total well-being as it is possible to perform in a sitting position with one's back against a door. I shook hands with myself, held up my thumb and index finger in the form of an O, and smiled even more emphatically.

'If you ask me, I think he's an escaped loonie,' said the second woman.

Iris Murdoch, *Under the Net*

I

Since nineteenth-century fiction consists very largely of conversations, interviews and arguments the typical page tends to be made up of dialogue interspersed with brief descriptive phrases that are in effect stage directions. The success of the great Victorians lay in their fluent and expressive handling of this mixed medium. Unluckily it is a medium very resistant, for purely technical reasons, to analytical study. The critic will always find it easier to quote and dissect an eloquent speech or a descriptive set-piece than to collate a series of scattered sentences and assess their cumulative effect. But for the sake of a fuller understanding of the workings of fiction the attempt should be made.

The minimal function of the simplest of these stage directions is to establish who says what. Without adequate signals of this kind the reader can get out of step, and allocate speeches mistakenly. But a deficiency of such signals is much less common than a seeming excess. The novelist is likely to insert 'said Smith' or 'replied Jones' at numerous points where the reader needs no such explanation. Usually the real function of these ostensibly ascriptive phrases is to control the pace and emphasis of the direct speech. Without them the dialogue could seem too rapid and glib, too much like verbal ping-pong. The speakers could appear implausibly quick-thinking and articulate. There would also be a likelihood of the reader misjudging shifts of mood, manner or inflection. To take a suitably slight example : ' "Isn't he very rich?" said Rebecca. "They say all Indian nabobs are enormously rich." ' The apparently redundant 'said Rebecca' hints at a change of tone. Becky Sharp, who has conceived the notion of hooking Joe Sedley, is not eagerly pursuing her rather too pointed question, but pretending to generalise it. If the author had been less confident he might have made the signal more obvious : 'asked Rebecca, eagerly; and added with a careless laugh . . .'. Thackeray could take the slight risk in the knowledge that novel-readers are accustomed to such small hints. The mature novelist only resorts to adverbs when he cannot contrive to imply them.

This introduction brings us into the subject very much at the shallow end. Stage directions, whether brief or extended, are the means by which the novelist gives substantiality to his dramatised scenes. Without such promptings these could dwindle, in the reader's apprehension, to toneless dialogues in space. There must be reminders that the characters have a physical dimension, and that the action is taking place *somewhere* – on a hill-top, in a drawing-room, at a railway station. A further general function of most stage directions is to convey a suitable sense of duration. The conversations that the novelist invents are more pointed and coherent and far briefer than the realities they mimic. His intermittent commentary relates to the component speeches as mortar relates to bricks : holding them apart as well as keeping them together. Just as the ten-minute interval in the theatre can somehow make more plausible a lapse of two years in the action of a play, so a number of brief descriptive phrases can dilate a passage of dialogue into something that will pass for equivalence with the time-scales of real life. In short, a set of interpolations with little or no descriptive usefulness can still serve a number of formal purposes.

But the concern of this chapter is specifically with *adverbial* comments of every kind – comments that show how, or in what circumstances, something is said. Descriptions of movement, posture or gesture will all be considered under this head.

Their immediate function, of course, is to authenticate and vivify the scenes in which they occur. A precisely recorded gesture can produce an effect similar to that of adjusting a pair of binoculars to make the general outlines of a distant view sharpen into detailed definition. The novelist's power of visualisation stimulates a corresponding imaginative energy in the reader. But, beyond this, descriptions of gesture can be made, cumulatively or even individually, a significant aspect of character portrayal. Obviously they can amplify what is spoken. A character may reveal by some action or movement an emotion he is unwilling to express, or is perhaps unaware of feeling. The inarticulate and the taciturn can be made to communicate by such a means. Even solitary behaviour can become expressive. The novelist can minimise the risk of seeming implausibly or arrogantly omniscient by thus implying the thought-processes of his characters rather than describing them directly. He gains, too, the usual advantages that suggestion holds over statement : he can avoid being too tidy or categorical.

But there remain difficulties with this technique at least as complex as those affecting the attempt to depict faces. Few would dispute that response to faces and facial expressions is an important factor in social relationships. There would be far less unanimity about the importance of gestures in general, and far less still about the significance of any particular gesture. Many of our small habitual movements seem random or inscrutable. Peacock's description of Scythrop implies another kind of difficulty : even if all these details are true to life and meaningful, do they hold *enough* meaning to justify the large number of words necessary to describe them? Many an actual gesture that communicates a good deal can only be represented verbally at a length disproportionate both to its importance and to the length of time it takes to enact.

The obverse of this difficulty is that a concise apt description of posture or gesture can give pleasure as a feat of wit. When Hardy writes : '. . . the reddleman waited in the window-bench of the kitchen, his hands hanging across his divergent knees, and his cap hanging from his hands', or 'At hearing him speak all the delicate activities in the young lady's person stood still : she stopped like a clock', the compact precision of the phrasing is as pleasing, in an unobtrusive way, as the psychological rightness. The great master of this art, of course, is Dickens. He records gesture with a stylistic vividness that seems a spontaneous reflex of his acuteness of observation.

It would hardly be feasible or desirable to write a novel in which every such detail was intrinsically striking : the effect would be too fussy and mannered. A few novelists – Jane Austen is an obvious example – show very little interest at all in gesture. But most of the great nineteenth-century authors found this a useful, even an important, kind of notation. For instance, George Eliot's tendency to concentrate too narrowly on the moral and intellectual life of her characters is greatly alleviated by her constant awareness of physical movements and mannerisms. Not only are individual scenes made more dramatic and visualisable, but we are also reminded that the characters concerned have bodies as well as souls and minds. A total lack of response to gesture on a novelist's part could be seen as a deficiency akin to colour blindness or tone deafness. Conversely, the writer who notices this or that small physical trait seems likely to be sensitive to other aspects of human conduct or psychology. A novelist's 'authority' is conventionally derived from his moral insight, wit, or breadth of sympathy; but surely acuteness of physical observation also wins an important kind of tacit respect from the reader?

II

This seems an appropriate place to say something about stage directions in general. Only a proportion of them, of course, are directly concerned with gesture, but a good deal of what appears to be scene-setting has a strong indirect relevance. Gesture demands physical context : chairs to sit in or rise from, windows to look out of, fires to stare into.

Accomplishment in this aspect of the novelist's art is extremely resistant to critical demonstration. To claim that a work is 'vividly imagined' or 'powerfully visual' is merely to toss a vague compliment in the right general direction. Extended descriptions of people or scenery are convenient for quotation and analysis, but they may have little bearing on the page-to-page texture of the dramatised scenes. And that is the issue : the mingling of dialogue and commentary that constitutes so large a proportion of most novels. The critic's problem here is almost insuperable. By definition the descriptive details concerned must be distributed along the length of an extended episode : a short episode would generate too few of them to be worth analysing. So there is the obvious difficulty of protracted quotation. Then, in their nature, these details will be intrinsically unremarkable, often unobtrusive. Their function is to subserve the dialogue, not to distract from it. An attempt to demonstrate, at considerable expense of words, that a series of tame, widely separated sentences has some sort of cumulative relevance and force is not an obviously promising critical enterprise. But here is such an attempt, kept, I hope, decently brief, and possibly the worse for it.

The passage to be discussed, from *Wives and Daughters*, cannot be appreciated without a reasonably full recollection of the context. Molly Gibson, the seventeen-year-old daughter of the local doctor, is staying at Hamley Hall, where Mrs Hamley is seriously ill. Squire Hamley refuses to see, or at any rate to acknowledge, the gravity of his wife's condition. One day Doctor Gibson tells Molly that he has sent to Cambridge for the two Hamley sons – Osborne, who has lately been in disgrace with his parents for failing exams and running up debts, and Roger. The clear implication is that Mrs

Hamley is dying. Doctor Gibson asks Molly to break this news to
the Squire. She does so that evening, after dinner :

The great log was placed on the after-dinner fire, the hearth
swept up, the ponderous candles snuffed, and then the door was
shut and Molly and the Squire left to their dessert. She sat at
the side of the table in her old place. That at the head was
vacant; yet, as no orders had been given to the contrary, the
plate and glasses and napkin were always arranged as regularly
and methodically as if Mrs Hamley would come in as usual.
Indeed, sometimes, when the door by which she used to enter was
opened by any chance, Molly caught herself looking round as if
she expected to see the tall languid figure in the elegant draperies
of rich silk and soft lace, which Mrs Hamley was wont to wear
of an evening.

This evening, it struck her, as a new thought of pain,that into
that room she would come no more. She had fixed to give her
father's message at this very point of time; but something in her
throat choked her, and she hardly knew how to govern her voice.
The Squire got up and went to the broad fireplace, to strike into
the middle of the great log, and split it up into blazing, sparkling
pieces. His back was towards her. Molly began, 'When papa was
here today, he bade me tell you he had written to Mr Roger
Hamley to say that – that he thought he had better come home;
and he enclosed a letter to Mr Osborne Hamley to say the same
thing.'

The Squire put down the poker, but he still kept his back to
Molly.

'He sent for Osborne and Roger?' he asked at length.

Molly answered, 'Yes.'

Then there was a dead silence, which Molly thought would
never end. The Squire had placed his two hands on the high
chimney-piece, and stood leaning over the fire.

'Roger would have been down from Cambridge on the 18th,'
said he. 'And he has sent for Osborne, too ! Did you know,' he
continued, turning round to Molly, with something of the fierce-
ness she had anticipated in voice and look. In another moment
he had dropped his voice. 'It's right, quite right. I understand.
It has come at length. Come ! come ! Osborne has brought it on,
though,' with a fresh access of anger in his tones. 'She might
have' (some word Molly could not hear – she thought it sounded
like 'lingered') 'but for that. I can't forgive him; I cannot.'

And then he suddenly left the room. While Molly sat there

still, very sad in her sympathy with all, he put his head in again :
    'Go to her, my dear; I cannot – not just yet. But I will soon.
Just this bit; and after that I won't lose a moment. You're a good
girl. God bless you !'

This passage constitutes the complete scene. If that scene comes
to life for us, if we are led to dramatise it, visualise it, if we infer
mood or motive from what is described, the cause lies in the author's
mastery of her mixed medium. Close reading should show how she
achieves most of her effects.

Molly is nervous about giving her message. On earlier occasions
the Squire has been 'almost savage' at suggestions that Mrs
Hamley's condition is worsening. If, through fear or grief, she fails
to control her voice, she may not be able to say what she needs to
say, or may say it too crudely. The Squire's move to the fireplace
eases her task by enabling her to speak when his back is towards
her. The stage direction is not incidental : it tells us something
about Molly.

The multiple stages of the Squire's reaction are expressed not
only in his words, but also in his four changes of tone, in his movements, and in the silences which those movements help to define.
He digests the news, reads its full implications, feels shock and grief
and then an instinctive anger, directed first against Molly herself
and then against Osborne. His continued reluctance to believe that
his wife is dying is dramatised by the two pauses : the first when he
puts down the poker, and the second after Molly's final 'Yes'. He
stands leaning over the fire because he cannot face her until he has
taken in what he has been told and gained command over his
feelings. Again the stage direction is only apparently a matter of
mere physical movement. His reappearance after leaving the room
shows that he can master himself, as he says he will, and that even
in his grief he feels a need to show appreciation of Molly's loyalty.

This fairly obvious commentary spells out a series of inferences
that a reader would draw almost unthinkingly, in much the same
way as he would read and respond to a situation in his own life.
Mrs Gaskell's account of this sad moment conveys in a variety of
ways the confused feelings of a shy girl and a proud, irascible man.
Their speeches are convincingly phrased, convincingly *heard* –
especially the Squire's short, shifting, jerky sentences. But his
gestures and pauses, and Molly's inability to speak one phrase of the
sympathy she feels, communicate as much as their words.

The setting, too, is made to contribute to the significance of the
scene. This dining-room has been described before, at the time of

Molly's first visit to the Hamleys, when she finds its size and bareness oppressive, and the formal dinner 'wearisome'. A recollection of that earlier scene adds to the poignancy of this one. This is a setting in which we have seen the Squire happily at home, protected by ritual and habit. On the earlier occasion Mrs Hamley was present, though already showing signs of her illness. Molly's task is the harder in that she must tackle the Squire in the room in which he is most confident and yet most vulnerable. A few months after making her first nervous visit she must take command, and break crucial news that spells the end of the ordered Hamley life that once awed her. She realises, as the Squire must, that his wife will never set foot in the room again.

This seems to me a moving scene; but its virtues elude most of the familiar kinds of critical inquiry. The incident is a sad, but not a tragic one. It contributes only indirectly to the larger action of the novel : Mrs Hamley is only a minor character. Molly and the Squire are likeable, but not particularly 'interesting'. They say nothing striking. The setting is adequately evoked, but is unremarkable. There is no symbolic suggestion in the scene, or any sort of deeper meaning. The author does not intervene with a wise observation. Yet merely to praise the scene as 'honest' or 'sensitive' is not enough. There are at least two subtler merits here. In this episode, as generally in *Wives and Daughters*, small congruities of character, conversational manner, gesture, topography, life-style reassure us that these people, these places, these lives have been solidly imagined, are steadily present in the author's mind. The characters say no more than their intelligence or temperament would allow them to say. The dining-room is not invented to accommodate the scene : the scene shapes itself to the pre-existent reality of the dining-room. In a dozen small ways the episode contributes to a feeling of sustained imaginative consistency in the novel, such that we do not merely accept, but positively believe in, the story.

The simplicity of the characters and the restraint of the narrator preclude striking psychological insights. But in no other way could the communications of people not particularly fluent but decently concerned with the feelings and responses of others be truthfully related. What the medium does enable Mrs Gaskell to display is a capacity that is surely of major importance to the novelist : she knows how people behave. And to tell us how a character would behave in a given situation is perhaps a more demanding feat, because so much more easily judged in terms of the reader's own day-to-day observations, than the more generally praised achievement of telling us how the character would think.

III

Is it useful or even possible to generalise about gestures in fiction, and about what they may be made to express? The following discussion will take its bearings from the two extreme positions theoretically possible : one, that the enormous majority of gestures, in novels as in life, are so random and ambiguous as to communicate nothing of interest; the other, that there is a coherent language of gesture, a language instinctively spoken by all of us, that the novelist can consciously manipulate and the critic learn to interpret.

Manifestly there are certain small everyday actions – nods, waves, winks, yawns – to which we ascribe a meaning without hesitation. Other gestures as plainly strive after meaning : 'Maggy shook her head, made a drinking vessel of her clenched left hand, drank out of it, and said, "Gin".' Little Dorrit's friend, mentally stunted, uses mime to eke out her small stock of words. Any novelist who describes a character engaging in solitary activity implies that the activity is somehow expressive. It is possible to write a short story (Hemingway's 'Big Two-Hearted River' is an example) consisting of nothing *but* gesture.

Yet these simple illustrations already imply three quite distinct categories of possible meaning. The nod or the wink is a conventional signal; Maggy invents an action to express an idea she cannot verbalise; Nick Adams is not attempting to communicate at all – he has no one to communicate with – but the reader is expected to see significance in his actions. Gesture is not one language, but a system of languages.

The quickest and most convenient way into a complex subject would be an examination of the practice of an individual author. Dickens is the great observer and inventor of gesture. A brief discussion should be sufficient to suggest how diversely functional and expressive is this aspect of his work.

Some of the most entertaining gestures he describes seem to have been included largely, or even solely, for their intrinsic oddity. Mr Fips devouring his piece of horsehair, Mr Stryver tapping a tune on his teeth with a ruler, Mantalini putting a sovereign in one eye and winking with the other are not so much revealing their individual personalities as testifying to the variousness and peculiarity of human conduct. There is pleasure in such testimony – a pleasure sufficiently intricate to merit a little analysis. In *Beyond the Fringe* Jonathan Miller referred to 'those little personal things that people sometimes do when they think they're alone in railway carriages – things like smelling their own armpit'. Why is the remark funny? Why was the laughter it aroused not only noisy but prolonged? Perhaps because reaction ran through several stages : recognition (Yes, people do such things – I have myself'); embarrassment ('My laughter betrays my personal experience of this dubious deed'); relief ('But everyone else is laughing, too. We've all done it!'); speculation ('Why do we do such things? Why are we not consciously aware that we do them?'). As the laughter subsided, Jonathan Miller summed up for the audience : 'I suppose it's all part of the human condition.' The odder gestures in Dickens tend to be familiar rather in kind than in themselves – we are convicted armpit-sniffers, while only potential horsehair-eaters – but they are similarly comments on the human condition. As such, they have a double function. The epic-writer claimed attention by describing the remarkable deeds of heroes. The novelist, who has the harder task of dealing with familiar situations and 'ordinary' people, can yet vivify them by showing how much of the extraordinary we take for granted in everyday life. Dickens repeatedly entertains us with displays of just this kind. At the same time he is widening the whole scope of his novels. In a world where such small freaks of behaviour are freely observable but often pass unnoticed, *this* degree of filial love, *that* degree of envy, hyprocrisy or obsession may also flourish unsuspected.

Yet there is a category of gesture in Dickens that has nothing to do with everyday realities. Throughout his career as a novelist he shows a willingness to allow his characters, in extreme situations, to react and speak in accordance with the conventions of the melodramatic stage. Notoriously the most curious exhibit here is *Nicholas Nickleby.* In the Vincent Crummles episodes Dickens extracts some pleasant comedy from the posturings of the troupe, both on and off the stage. Yet in the serious parts of the narrative the characters often attitudinise no less extravagantly. Sir Mulberry Hawk, in the grip of passion, 'could not articulate, but stood clenching his fist, tearing his hair, and stamping upon the ground'. Why should the reader not laugh at Sir Mulberry, or at Ralph Nickleby, as he does at Lenville or Crummles? In his other novels Dickens does not aggravate by satire the problems inherent in his use of melodramatic convention; but the problems remain, and sometimes obtrude. All the great Victorian novelists modulate more or less uneasily into melodrama on occasion. Dickens makes the task harder for himself by his preoccupation with gesture. In *Little Dorrit* several of the major characters are virtually defined by this means. Merdle has little existence beyond his physical mannerisms.

William Dorrit's stately deportment is betrayed by the throat-
clearing, by the straying of the 'irresolute hand' to the 'trembling
lips'. His longer and more devious speeches carry a physical
commentary :

> While he spoke, he was opening and shutting his hands like
> valves. . . .
>
> All this time, though he had finished his supper, he was nervously
> going about his plate with his knife and fork, as if some of it were
> still before him.

Such details are powerfully realistic, and they prompt the reader to
see. In the context they help to create and sustain melodramatic
moments stand out awkwardly. Little Dorrit, hearing that her
brother has been imprisoned for debt, 'cried, with her clasped hands
lifted above her head, that it would kill their father if he ever knew
it; and fell down at Tip's graceless feet'. When Mrs Clennam
repents she kneels to Little Dorrit and kisses her dress. As usual,
Dickens invites us to visualise; but here we see waxwork tableaux
instead of living scenes – that is, if we see anything at all. The
qualification is important : many of Dickens's melodramatic scenes
are starkly posed – may, indeed, be starkly depicted by his illustrator
– but remain strangely unvisualisable. On the eve of her wedding
Edith Granger paces her room : 'with her dark hair shaken down,
her dark eyes flashing with a raging light, her broad white bosom
red with the cruel grasp of the relentless hand with which she
spurned it from her . . .'. The gesture here, surely, is purely verbal,
and the reader's imaginative response accordingly vague. We do not
'see' Edith spurning her bosom as we 'see' Merdle 'fitting a table-
spoon up his sleeve'. All this is not to deny that Dickens could and
did make effective use of melodramatic gesture in his novels. The
problem for him was that in this area of description he moved
between extreme realism and extreme stylisation. The melodramatic
gestures became less assimilable as his art developed and engaged
more directly with the social and psychological stresses of his time.
Edith Dombey and Mr Merdle do not speak the same physical
language.

George Sampson, the friend of the Wilfer family, is by no means
the only character in Dickens who thrusts the head of his stick into
his mouth.. Others include Lord Verisopht, Jonas Chuzzlewit and
Dick Swiveller. Contemporary sketches and paintings suggest that
this practice was not uncommon, but do not tell us what, if anything, it signified, or how it was regarded. It is obviously likely to

appear grotesque to the modern reader because walking-sticks and
canes are in such short supply. A wide range of Victorian gestures
involved accoutrements that have now disappeared or become very
scarce : hats, gloves, fans, monocles, parasols, snuff-boxes, pocket-
watches, beards. Within the very recent past the handkerchief that
could be drawn forth with a flourish to mop the brow has become
an endangered species. Mr Peggotty would never have covered the
face of the fallen Em'ly with a Kleenex. The novelist of today has
to overwork the few trappings that remain : handbags, pipes,
cigarettes and cigarette-lighters. A whole genre of deportment was
eliminated when the horse gave way to the motor-car. Driving-styles
are a pallid substitute for riding-styles, and the driver carries no
equivalent to the riding-crop. Equipment aside, fashions in gesture
have changed. We shake hands less often, bow or curtsey hardly at
all. Men no longer shed tears or link arms. In terms of class and
social convention Dickens's novels are so remote from our experience
that we are liable to misread his finer detail, to overlook or misconstrue carefully recorded snubs, blunders, unorthodoxies.

The danger is particularly marked in relation to etiquette – the
whole troublesome business of when to sit and when to stand in
company, of how to dispose of one's hat or one's hands when
addressing a social superior. The performance or non-performance
of gestures of this kind can convey a great variety of meanings.
Erving Goffman makes sociological capital of the passage in *The
Portrait of a Lady* in which the mere fact that Madame Merle is
standing and Gilbert Osmond sitting as they converse suggests to
Isabel that they have been lovers.[11] Without James's own commentary on the scene this is an inference that the modern reader
would probably miss. Usually the buried suggestions are far slighter,
but they can still be important to the reader's general grasp of
character and situation. The modern student can too easily dismiss
Joe Gargery's deportment before Miss Havisham as merely imbecilic,
or fail to see the full offensiveness of Sir Mulberry Hawk's drawing
Kate Nickleby's 'arm through his up to the elbow' within a few
minutes of first meeting her. An active sense of what was or wasn't
'done' in Victorian England is a great help towards a full appreciation of Dickens. But just as the inference about Madame Merle and
Gilbert Osmond involves not only etiquette but also a variety of
other kinds of information about the characters concerned, so, too,
in Dickens, the courtesy offered or neglected acquires meaning in
relation to particular personalities or situations. F. R. Leavis draws
attention to Glennam's courtesy, as remarked upon by Mrs
Plornish : 'It ain't many that comes into a poor place, that deems

it worth their while to move their hats. . . . But people think more
of it than people think.'¹² Glennam is as instinctively polite to a
plasterer's wife as he would be to a society lady. Mr Plornish has
earlier shown a comparable delicacy, in a situation for which the
rules of etiquette could make no provision. The Father of the
Marshalsea 'feebly burst into tears' when Plornish made the mistake
of giving him a 'testimonial' of copper coins; and 'The Plasterer
turned him towards the wall, that his face might not be seen . . .'.

The numerous courtesy-gestures in Dickens are essentially significant in so far as they do or do not express sincere good feeling. No
novelist makes his characters shake hands so often. Mr Toots and
Mr Dick, for instance, are constantly at it, as though here was a
physical means of working off an excess of good fellowship. Yet
Dickens is at pains to show that a handshake can be made to express
far less agreeable qualities: sycophancy, condescension, or even
hostility. The fact is that *no* gesture has absolute value for Dickens.
Pickwick, Tom Pinch and the Cheeryble brothers are all given to
rubbing their hands. One might reasonably deduce that for their
creator this gesture seemed indicative of kindliness and innocent
zest. But two other persistent hand-rubbers are Quilp, who is
zestful but evil, and Uriah Heep, who is evil and insidious. Plainly,
as with Gowan's stone-kicking, it is not the action itself but the
manner of it that is revealing. In these instances the manner no
doubt has something to do with the quality of the hands being
rubbed. Uriah Heep's are clammy, requiring stealthy drying on his
pocket handkerchief, while Quilp's are so filthy that his hand-
rubbing generates little pellets of dirt. The habit is coloured by the
character concerned as much as the character is coloured by the
habit.

As Dickens became increasingly concerned with the continuity
and coherence of his novels he tended to use descriptive detail for
structural purposes, making it a means of linking one part of the
narrative to other parts. Gesture is frequently so used. Mr Omer,
the asthmatic undertaker who makes four widely separated appearances in *David Copperfield*, provides a conveniently simple illustration. Although David meets him so seldom, he plays a useful
connecting role in the novel. He buries David's father, mother and
brother, and later Barkis, and is Em'ly's employer. As David's few
other East Anglian acquaintances die or move away, Mr Omer
provides continuity – a particularly steady character, full of local
news and old memories. But since there is so little for him to *do*, his
personality becomes a matter of words and mannerisms. It so
happens that, although Mr Omer is wholly amiable, his most

obvious gestures are associated with some of Dickens's 'bad' characters. He rubs his chin, as does Uriah Heep; he laughs himself into near-fatal attacks of coughing, as does Major Bagstock. The intimate way in which he touches David's waistcoat with forefinger or pipe recalls the evil Marquis in *A Tale of Two Cities*: 'Once again he touched him on the breast, as though his finger were the fine point of a small sword, with which, in delicate finesse, he ran him through the body. . . .' So, again, the gestures have no intrinsic meaning : they seem genial because Mr Omer is genial. They are not particularly striking : Mr Omer is a very ordinary man. But they are sufficiently noticeable to bring swiftly back to the reader's recollection a character who has not been seen, perhaps, for two hundred pages – several months, in terms of the original serial publication. If Mr Omer were deprived of his mannerisms he would barely exist. He holds the Yarmouth episodes together, and is himself held together by his gestures.

Such an example may seem too slight, and too bound up with Dickens's habitual method of character-portrayal, to shed much light on questions of structure. But it at least furnishes an introduction to them. Thanks to his gestures Mr Omer remains recognisable from episode to episode, and therefore provides a useful link between David's past and present. As we read Chapter 30 we are led to recall Chapter 21, or Chapter 9. His gestures hark back, as little Em'ly's run along the protruding timber, above the deep water, harks forward. The reader is insensibly drawn to see the novel not as a sequence of events, merely, but as a system of inter-relationships. In the later novels the means by which Dickens contrives to connect any one part of his narrative with many others become far more elaborate; and gesture is one such means. When Joe Gargery first comes to visit Pip in London : 'he caught both my hands and worked them straight up and down, as if I had been the last-patented Pump'. Earlier this warmth has been parodied by an opportunist :

'My dear friend,' said Mr Pumblechook, taking me by both hands, when he and I and the collation were alone, 'I give you joy of your good fortune. Well deserved, well deserved !'

The meal, of course, is punctuated by a whole series of effusive handshakes. By contrast Wemmick has so lost the habit of shaking hands that he scarcely remembers that other people still maintain it. He himself reserves that salutation for the aged parent and for those about to be executed. Mr Jaggers is 'always a remarkably short shaker', but his large hands are otherwise much in evidence : he gnaws his forefinger, and has a trick of throwing it in the direction of a man he is interrogating. He washes his hands very carefully at the end of each day's dubious work. When Magwitch reappears his 'favourite action', which he frequently repeats, is to reach out both his hands to take Pip's. The reader who has been responding alertly to the novel will have become sufficiently sensitive to the quality of such gestures to perceive that at first the convict is not showing the pure affection of Joe Gargery. His action can have a proprietorial, a Pumblechookian air :

> 'And this,' said he, dandling my hands up and down in his, as he puffed at his pipe; 'and this is the gentleman what I made ! The real genuine One ! It does me good fur to look at you, Pip.'

But later his pride of ownership and Pip's horrified sense of duty give way to love. On the boat back to London, and again at the trial, and again in the prison hospital Pip sits holding Magwitch's hand :

> Sometimes he was almost, or quite, unable to speak; then, he would answer me with slight pressures on my hand, and I grew to understand his meaning very well.

This recalls Wemmick's similarly silent communication, through violent nods, with the stone-deaf Aged. In both cases words have become useless, but a true affection is expressed through gesture alone. Pip's false pride has gone. His own illness reunites him with Gargery : 'Joe's eyes were red when I next found him beside me; but I was holding his hand and we both felt happy.'

These gestures borrow meaning from one another, and also from details of a rather different kind. Pip's alienation from his home and from Joe begins when he is made to feel ashamed of his own 'coarse hands'. At the climax of his troubles he badly burns both hands when trying to rescue Miss Havisham from the fire. The point I am trying to make is emphatically not that hands are 'symbolic' in *Great Expectations*, though it could involve a diluted version of such a claim. What Dickens has done, by instinct or design, or more probably by both, has been to limit, to harmonise, to cross-relate all sorts of subordinate descriptive detail, normally left random, in such a way as to link scene with scene and to reinforce his larger themes. From the virtually numberless possibilities open to him he regularly elects to concentrate on certain activities, certain features only. I have been concerned here with hands and hand-shakes. Barbara Hardy has shown how, and why, *Great Expectations* is structured round a long sequence of meals.[13] There are similar accounts to be written about boots, fires, money, mud, mist, reading and writing. Such recurrence trains the reader's eye, encourages him to see relationships, to draw comparisons, between character and character, episode and episode. Echoes and correspondences lead him to discern in Pip's experiences the patterns that Pip himself discerns. And the very moral of the book is in these patterns. A courtesy or a kindness here defines a discourtesy or an unkindness there. Envy or pretentiousness at one class-level are parodied at another. Characters socially remote prove to be intimately connected. Gesture is at once an aspect of Dickens's system of relationships, and a clue to its workings.

The commonest function of gesture, of course, is to reveal character. Dickens sometimes carries this technique to a hyperbolic extreme. Quilp's ally, Tom Scott, appears to express his personality almost solely through standing on his head, the Fat Boy through eating and sleeping. But he will often give a major character a whole range of gestures that collectively reveal his mind and temperament to the reader. The intention, the assumption, is that one such mannerism will shed light on another. There may be no common language of gesture, but the reader can be brought to understand the private dialect of a particular individual. The next two sections will try to show how fluently and suggestively two great novelists, Eliot and Dickens, make use of this technique.

IV

And why is he always grasping his coat-collar, as if he wished to hang himself up? The author had an uncomfortable feeling that she must make him do something real, something visible and sensible, and she hit upon that clumsy figure.[14]

Henry James, speaking through Pulcheria, is right about Daniel Deronda's characteristic gesture. It is inexpressive in itself, and extrinsic to Deronda's personality, such as that is. Eliot no doubt felt a need to reinforce her hero's physical presence in this way since most of the other major characters in her novel are distinctive in posture or movements. There is a constant stress on this kind of physical detail. Even in the crucial interview between Gwendolen and Klesmer, where both speakers are open and fluent, and where she herself claims the right to explain the workings of both minds, she writes in more than a score of stage directions, some of them quite elaborate. The tension and conflict of the encounter are partly enacted in the stance and movements of the characters. As was suggested earlier, the effect of this kind of writing is twofold : to vivify, to dramatise the scene, and to imply unspoken thoughts or feelings. Professor Leavis has emphasised how naturally and persuasively this kind of suggestion interacts with the words the characters say and with George Eliot's own particular mode of 'psychological notation'.[15] But it is the portrayal of Grandcourt that demonstrates most clearly how much may be conveyed through gesture, since in his case those other sources of information reveal little. It is essential that his actions speak louder than his words since he is so taciturn. Eliot even observes that he is 'not a wordy thinker'. She says comparatively little about the workings of his mind, partly, perhaps, because Grandcourt might not articulate them to himself, partly to ensure that he remains for the reader, as for Gwendolen, something of an unpredictable presence.

It is clear that Grandcourt cultivates a physical style, a manner, a stance, as a demonstration of his outlook. After his first meeting with Gwendolen he is shown in conversation with Klesmer :

. . . Grandcourt . . . listened with an impassive face and narrow eyes, his left fore-finger in his waistcoat-pocket, and his right slightly touching his thin whisker.

He is physically contrasted to Klesmer here, as later to Deronda; and in both cases the contrast extends to attitudes and even values. His impassivity is a silent criticism of the musician's animation and volubility. It is Grandcourt's habit to imply his superiority to enthusiasm or strong feeling by appearing ostentatiously untouched by it. Repeatedly he is seen in this favourite stance, or in seated variants of it, an arm or a leg languidly propped. The characteristic gestures – the averted face, the cigar-smoking, the silences, the lowering of eyes or voice – so harmonise that the mention of any one of them recalls the others, and brings Grandcourt visually to life. Together, they come to imply an indolent but inflexible self-absorption, an unobtrusively implacable will – and so supply psycho-logical, as well as visual, reminders.

There is a suppressed tension between Grandcourt's languor and the energies and appetites that involved him in tiger-hunting and pig-sticking. It gives a sharper edge to the controlled cruelty he exercises against Lush, Mrs Glasher and his dogs. He enjoys power, and relishes the challenge to display it. Just before his final boat-trip he is described as 'feeling perfectly satisfied that he held his wife with bit and bridle'. Gwendolen's submission to him and fear of him are made wholly understandable :

That white hand of his which was touching his whisker was capable, she fancied, of clinging round her neck and threatening to throttle her. . . .

She puts the threat in melodramatic terms, but the reality is hardly less sinister : Grandcourt *is* killing her morally and emotionally. He married her because she challenged him, and now he has defeated her.

Grandcourt and Gwendolen are in some sense in conflict from their very first encounter; and given his reticence the battle is necessarily carried on through small physical skirmishes : Will Gwendolen dance with him? Will he ask her to? Will he hold her burnous for her? Will she consent to put it on? Does she lose her whip on purpose? Will she allow him a kiss? To avoid physical contact she occupies her hands with her needlework, her gloves or her whip. On their wedding-day journey she turns 'his gentle seizure of her hand into a grasp of his hand by both hers, with an increased vivacity as of a kitten that will not sit quiet to be petted'. Eventually a context is created in which even a bitter quarrel need involve no spoken word :

She turned into the drawing-room, lest he should follow her farther and give her no place to retreat to; then sat down with a weary air, taking off her gloves, rubbing her hand over her forehead, and making his presence as much of a cipher as possible. But he sat too, and not far from her – just in front, where to avoid looking at him must have the emphasis of effort.

Gwendolen uses gestures that must have kept many an undesirable acquaintance at arm's length in the past. But her husband easily sustains his subtle cruelty and dominance. The mannerisms that have been Eliot's means of portraying him both physically and psychologically become weapons in a wordless conflict that powerfully implies the tensions of the Grandcourts' intimate life.

There is yet a further significance in this physical style. It has at first an attractiveness for Gwendolen that reveals an important aspect of her temperament. The girl who flinches from a kiss, who cries to Rex 'Pray don't make love to me! I hate it,' finds Grandcourt's manner reassuring. His way of offering his arm, opening a

door for her, putting her hand to his lips is all delicacy and discre-
tion : '. . . Grandcourt's behaviour as a lover had hardly at all
passed the limit of an amorous homage which was unobtrusive as
a wafted odour of roses, and spent all its effect in a gratified vanity.
. . . His reticence gave her some inexplicable, delightful consciousness.'

The suggestions involved here are too various to be simply spelt
out, but they include a hint of sexual frigidity on Gwendolen's part.
Ironically this helps to draw her into relationship with a man whose
apparent physical fastidiousness masks sadism and a desire to
humiliate. Her admiration for Grandcourt's manner is symptomatic
of a confusion of values, social and moral; but the punishment is
neatly implicit in the sin. Gwendolen thinks that the physical con-
sequences of marrying without love will be minimised by lack of
appetite or lack of insistence on her husband's part, and mollified by
decorum and elegance. She would suffer for this self-deception even
if Mrs Glasher did not exist.

George Eliot's handling of gesture is always interesting. But it is
a particularly striking achievement to make a character's physical
style reveal not just a great deal about himself, but also a great deal
about someone else.

V

Grandcourt has consciously cultivated what he judges to be the
demeanour of a gentleman. His mannerisms may be coloured by his
own indolence and insolence, but in themselves they are typical, not
idiosyncratic. Indeed, one of Grandcourt's functions is to be a
representative, if an extreme one, of an English 'style' that George
Eliot wishes to question. Dickens often shows a similar interest in
conscious deportment, Turveydrop being an obvious case in point;
but he is at his most interesting when he deals in gestures that are
not imitative but involuntary, and display the workings of the sub-
conscious. He can go far towards dramatising an entire personality
by such means.

Uriah Heep is an inviting example to consider, because no other
character in Dickens reveals himself so consistently and eloquently
through his gestures. He rubs his hands together, wipes them
stealthily on a handkerchief, fondles his chin. Repeatedly he
'writhes', 'undulates', 'jerks' with his entire person. When he stands
he is liable to draw up one leg; when he sits, to twist a foot round
the opposite calf. His general physical gracelessness is highlighted
by odd grimaces :

He left off scraping his chin, and sucked in his cheeks until they seemed to meet inside; keeping his sidelong glance upon me all the while.

Even his humour is grotesque :

Uriah stopped short, put his hands between his great knobs of knees, and doubled himself up with laughter. With perfectly silent laughter. Not a sound escaped from him.

Heep's mere appearance is described, or alluded to, again and again : red hair, cropped to stubble; red-brown eyes that lack brows or lashes; long, clammy, skeletal hands; splay feet; thin, pointed, 'twinkling' nostrils; a bony high-shouldered body. It is easy to forget the risk that Dickens runs in offering so elaborate, so bizarre and so insistent a portrayal. If these numerous physical attributes fail to appear harmonious, to be somehow mutually sustaining, the characterisation will seem the clumsiest patchwork, a desperate accumulation of random details. Needless to say, Dickens brings it off. The face, the physique, the posture, the mannerisms are wonderfully homogeneous, as a number of actors have been able to show in dramatisations. Here is a body-dialect that can be readily understood. 'Phiz' could soon improvise in it. His illustration 'Somebody Turns Up' shows Heep, who is presiding over tea, tightly clutching the table-leg between his thighs and ankles. The detail has no basis in the text, but 'takes' perfectly. A later illustration, with equal felicity, has Uriah warmly clasping David in a left-handed handshake.

But *why* does the portrayal work? What kind of logic informs it? These are not easy questions to answer. Some of Dickens's most striking characters are founded on recognisable physical types. Everyone has known a plethoric man, something like Major Bagstock, and a thin restless man, something like Jingle. Uriah Heep is less easy to place. I can't myself recall meeting anyone of quite this general physical make-up, though Dickens certainly persuades me that it can exist. But it can be said of Uriah that various of his characteristics inter-relate in a plausible, even in a probable, way. Some red-haired people observably have red-brown eyes. The absence of brows and lashes suggests an unhealthy state of hair that might reasonably lead to cropping the head. A man with damp cold hands is likely to warm or dry them in a Heep-like manner. A man who continually writhes his body will probably fidget also with his hands and feet.

There is a similar consistency at the psychological level. Uriah's cringing and wriggling are expressions of his desire to propitiate. He stirs his coffee 'softly' in order not to disturb. He laughs silently because he is sly. Altogether investigation confirms what the reader instinctively apprehends, that Heep's mannerisms make perfect sense. And, of course, scores of Dickens's characterisations make sense in just this way. What might be taken, at first sight, to be an arbitrary conjunction of eccentric gestures, garments, speech-habits proves, on analysis, to present a coherent psychological pattern.

So much I take to be pretty familiar. But the portrayal of Heep has a further dimension, of a curious kind. He is a sort of visual pun. His physique and movements represent his evilness in almost literal terms. He 'twists' because he is a twister, who can 'corkscrew' information out of the immature Copperfield. His hands are so clammy that his finger seems to leave a snail-like trail on the page he reads. Appropriately, his manner, too, is 'slimy'. The metaphorical merges into the actual. A good deal of metaphor is lavished on Heep, much of it to do with the less agreeable animals. He is compared, for instance, with a snake, a fish, a frog, a bat, a fox and a baboon. Moral condemnation is implied through strenuous physical denigration.

It is important to remember that the denigration comes from David Copperfield, who, from the very first, is both fascinated and repelled by Heep. The fascination lingers, and the detestation becomes almost pathological. David feels contaminated by Heep's touch. He dreams of him several times. When Heep stays the night in his rooms David cannot resist studying the ugly sleeping body. Earlier he has thought to run him through with a red-hot poker; later he does strike him so hard in the face that a tooth has to be removed. The 'official' reading of the relationship must be that the degree of David's loathing is commensurate with the quite extraordinary nastiness of Heep; but another interpretation is theoretically possible : namely, that David exaggerates Heep's unpleasantness as a means of justifying a wildly disproportionate dislike. In such a case Heep's gestures, as described by David, would do more than contribute to a plausible physical portrait – they would reveal something about the portrayer.

This is a possibility that I will return to later, since it takes me too far from my immediate concerns. Whatever their secondary functions Heep's gestures have as their primary purpose the revelation of his personality – his whole personality. He has a complex of movements and mannerisms that imply a complex of psychological characteristics. If this is a common technique in Dickens's novels, there is a variant of it that is scarcely less common – the use of a singe habit or activity to signalise some particular emotional or psychological stress. The classic case, demanding to be looked at, is that of Dr Manette.

The superb opening of *A Tale of Two Cities* implies a connection between the worst horrors of pre-revolutionary France and the strange mission undertaken by Mr Lorry. That mission eventually brings him and the reader to the garret of Dr Manette. All that we see, at the close of five powerfully anticipatory chapters, is 'a white-haired man . . . very busy, making shoes'.

The shoe-making has to carry a tremendous weight of significance. It quickly transpires that Dr Manette has virtually no memory and even finds difficulty in speaking. His past sufferings and his present state of mind can only be inferred, dimly, from what he does. He has a number of characteristic gestures that derive from his imprisonment – for example, his trick, when addressed, of looking 'with a vacant air of listening, at the floor on one side of him; then similarly at the floor on the other side of him; then, upward at the speaker'. But the basic psychological disorder is conveyed through his shoe-making. This is the activity he needs and clings to, and would pursue incessantly if left to himself. Deprived of it, he resorts to aimless movements :

Now that he had no work to hold, he laid the knuckles of the right hand in the hollow of the left, and then the knuckles of the left hand in the hollow of the right, and then passed a hand across his bearded chin, and so on in regular changes, without a moment's intermission.

The carefulness of the description is true to the concentrated intentness of the whole episode. Dr Manette's shoe-making is shown to be central to his existence, and so becomes central to the reader's curiosity about the emerging story. Why does he do it? What lies behind it? What does it represent? All the considerable energy of the first book of the novel is focused on these questions. But Dickens postpones his answer. He carries his narrative abruptly five years forward, and shifts his attention to the Carton–Darnay story. Only gradually, and with extreme tact, does he revert to the problems posed in his opening chapters.

In Book the First the reader sees all that Mr Lorry sees. In Book the Second he is eventually acquainted with all that Mr Lorry has since learned – namely, that Dr Manette has recovered, but never alludes to his past, and still keeps the work-bench, unused, in his bedroom. His obsession is in abeyance, but has not been decisively cured. He still, on occasion, rises in the middle of the night and is heard 'walking up and down, walking up and down, in his room'. Dickens makes no direct comment on the situation, but he offers a preliminary diagnosis through Miss Pross. She suggests that Dr Manette is 'afraid of the whole subject' because :

> It's a dreadful remembrance. Besides that, his loss of himself grew out of it. Not knowing how he lost himself, or how he recovered himself, he may never feel certain of not losing himself again.

Later come the relapses : a brief one after Darnay has declared his love for Lucie, a much longer one after their wedding, which drives him back to his shoe-making for nine days. When he comes round Mr Lorry contrives the extraordinary scene in which Dr Manette is induced to pass judgment on his own case.

The whole conception is remarkable in its insight and development. What Dr Manette prescribed for himself in prison – 'I asked leave to teach myself, and I got it with much difficulty after a long while' – was a kind of work-therapy. The treatment was successful in that he remained sane; but it became itself an addiction, a problem in its own right. Although he recovers after his reunion with his daughter, he remains, and is aware that he remains, psychologically vulnerable. He keeps the work-bench as a stand-by : a return to his addiction would be preferable to mental collapse. When it has enabled him to survive the supreme test of his daughter's marriage, his triumph is to be able to pass judgment on his own case.

The scene of auto-diagnosis is a masterpiece. Dickens has shown a wonderful delicacy in moving from his first purely objective account of Dr Manette through the tentative speculations of Miss Pross and Mr Lorry to Manette's own explanation. Nothing could be more remote from authorial patronage than to let the mentally sick physician have the last word. Dickens makes no comments of his own. Dr Manette's account of his obsession shows the author's astonishing psychological acuity, and is sensitively phrased : '. . . no doubt it relieved his pain so much, by substituting the perplexity of the fingers for the perplexity of the brain, and by substituting, as he became more practised, the ingenuity of the hands for the ingenuity of the mental torture; that he has never been able to bear the thought of putting it quite out of his reach'. Also acute is the fact that Manette's acknowledgment of his problems to Mr Lorry becomes part of his treatment. It is true, of course, as he himself points out, that his survival of what seems to be a unique pressure towards relapse must give him confidence for the future. But the fact that he can now speak openly, or almost openly, is surely another reason for his courageous new willingness to have his work-bench destroyed.

It is a great convenience to Dickens as story-teller that Dr Manette's explanation is given merely in general psychological terms, thus obviating the more detailed account of his sufferings and their cause that the reader has long been expecting. This revelation is to be reserved for the very climax of the novel. It must be admitted that hereabouts is located a confusion, a duplicity of intention, that clouds not only the story of Dr Manette, but the whole novel. For the modern reader, at least, it is as though Dickens has been more psychologically subtle than his plot will permit. As we have seen, all the early narrative interest is concentrated on the extremely intriguing figure of Dr Manette. Here is a man who has been locked up for nearly eighteen years. The effects on him of imprisonment alone must have been so grave that further information about the *cause* of his incarceration, beyond confirmation of the fact that he was punished innocently, scarcely seems to matter. Manette's account of himself is perfectly compatible with the possibility that it was prolonged confinement alone that had preyed upon his mind and spirit. His mental sufferings are so finely imaged and explained that it seems natural to respond to his story, if not to the whole narrative, largely at the psychological level. But in fact the author has a plot to develop – a distinctly strained and laborious plot. It is to transpire that Dr Manette's relapses were not simply occasioned – as they well could have been, given his long experience of isolation – by the probability and later the actuality of his daughter's marriage. They relate to recollections concerning his arrest – recollections that constitute the thin thread linking the dramatic opening of the novel with its melodramatic close. When the truth is eventually revealed all the emphasis has been shifted to plot – to the probability of Darnay being executed. Dr Manette has been thrust to the margins of the story. Yet this trial scene should be a devastating ordeal for him. Earlier he has been 'exalted' to find that his imprisonment has proved in Paris to be a source of authority and strength. Now this power is swept away, his past sufferings are abruptly recalled, and he finds himself the involuntary betrayer of his son-in-law. It is scarcely surprising that he should soon be seeking his old work-bench again. Earlier in the novel this relapse would have been of crucial interest; now Dickens can hardly spare it a paragraph – he has too much other business on his hands.

Carton's final unspoken prophecy suggests that Manette will be again restored; but we last glimpse him as a 'helpless, inarticulately murmuring, wandering old man'. Dickens's profounder concerns have been crowded out by trivial ones.

The psychological study that Dickens thus lightly abandons has an interesting part to play in the economy of the novel as a whole. Dr Manette's story shows violent stress giving way to drastic cure; it is not remote from the contemporary history of France. There is hardly a major character in the book who does not to some extent reflect his duality of nature. Carton, Darnay, Cly, Monsieur and Madame Defarge – each has a concealed aspect of personality. In the case of Madame Defarge suppression is revealed and expressed through physical work, as it is with Dr Manette. As he makes shoes, so she knits. It would be a mistake to look for some profound metaphorical pattern in these resemblances. Like the controlled descriptive detail in *Great Expectations* they encourage the reader to understand the novel as a single coherent entity, to seek meaning in the inter-relationship of all its parts.

There are characters elsewhere in Dickens who ease distress or mental confusion by some kind of physical activity. Tommy Traddles, daily chastised at Salem House, finds solace in drawing skeletons. Mr Toots, when his mind fails, writes himself numerous letters, as from important people. The case of Mr Dick is a more complex one, because he has not one but three modes of self-protection. The memory of his sufferings being oppressive to him, he speaks not of them but of King Charles the First : 'He connects his illness with great disturbance and agitation, naturally, and that's the figure, or the simile, or whatever it's called, which he chooses to use.' For more than ten years he has been preparing a Memorial about his affairs for the Lord Chancellor, and struggling vainly to keep it free of references to King Charles. It is plain that the Memorial will never be completed, but 'it keeps him employed'. When the Memorial itself gets too much for him he makes a gigantic kite of its pages and flies it to a great height. The image of Mr Dick with his kite is a very beautiful one, particularly to anyone who has wrestled with the composition of a book or thesis. Thanks to these devices and the care of Betsey Trotwood, a man who has spent some time in an asylum is able to lead a contented, even a useful, life.

A fictional ancestor of these characters is Tristram Shandy's Uncle Toby, who forgets the pain of his war-wound in eagerly reconstructing the battle at which he received it. In each of these cases a sad experience, which could have been painful to hear about, has been rendered tolerable to the person concerned, and hence to the reader.

There is optimism here – a tribute to human resilience and resource-fulness.

The history of Dr Manette makes it clear that, if at one extreme Dickens delighted to record random mannerisms for their intrinsic oddity, at the other he was a conscious and brilliant interpreter of gesture. The diagnosis Dickens supplies through Doctor Manette himself sanctions the reader to seek comparable psychological complexities in the gestures of Merdle or Jaggers or Headstone. Such portraits could not, of course, be isolated exercises; deportment can only be made expressive in a fictional context in which posture and mannerism are habitually described. Only because most of the characters in *Little Dorrit* have gestures of some kind can Merdle have meaningful gestures. Dickens regularly implies that we are, or should be, automatically aware of the ways in which people stand, or sit, or move. In ordinary daily life such details might be mildly suggestive; in exceptional circumstances they could be deeply revealing. Psychological diagnosis can be seen as an extreme extension of the normal habits of social observation. In this aspect of his work as in others Dickens teaches us to understand by teaching us to see.

VI

In Chapter XXVI of *Bleak House*, after a preliminary paragraph concerning the gamesters and other seedy denizens of the Leicester Square neighbourhood, Dickens gives a lengthy account of Mr George's morning ablutions :

Mr George, having shaved himself before a looking-glass of minute proportions, then marches out, bare-headed and bare-chested, to the Pump, in the little yard, and anon comes back shining with yellow soap, friction, drifting rain, and exceedingly cold water. As he rubs himself upon a large jack-towel, blowing like a military sort of diver just come up : his crisp hair curling tighter and tighter on his sun-burnt temples, the more he rubs it, so that it looks as if it could never be loosened by any less coercive instrument than an iron rake or a curry-comb – as he rubs, and puffs, and polishes, and blows, turning his head from side to side, the more conveniently to excoriate his throat, and standing with his body well bent forward, to keep the wet from his martial legs – Phil, on his knees lighting a fire, looks round as if it were enough washing for him to see all that done, and sufficient renovation, for one day, to take in the superfluous health his master throws off.

Both Esther Summerson and the omniscient narrator characterise Mr George largely through posture and gesture. He is regularly seen to pass his hand across his forehead, to fold his arms across his chest, to smoke a pipe, to press his palm against his upper lip. But in particular he stands, walks, and even sits, like a soldier :

> What is curious about him is, that he sits forward on his chair as if he were, from long habit, allowing space for some dress or accoutrements that he has altogether laid aside.

It is appropriate to a man who has come from, and is to return to, the world of Sir Leicester Dedlock that his style, physical and moral, should be, for all its admirable qualities, the product of a formal picturesque mode of life that has been abandoned. George is an *ex*-soldier : his posture and movements are adjusted to a uniform that he no longer wears. He smooths the lip that used to sport a military moustache.

But that much is merely qualification. The essential, and deliberately simple, metaphorical statement that is being made about George is that he is a healthy, upright, disciplined man. His physical ease and energy are in permanent contrast to the frailty, ill health and unhealthiness visible at so many social and occupational levels – in Krook, in Miss Flite, in Jo, in Sir Leicester, in Vholes, in Gride, in Richard, in the Smallweeds. The 'superfluous health' that gives strength to Phil Squod seems positively to threaten annihilation to the Smallweeds :

> As he sits in the middle of the grim parlour, leaning a little forward, with his hands upon his thighs and his elbows squared, he looks as though, if he remained there long, he would absorb into himself the whole family and the whole four-roomed house, extra little back-kitchen and all.

The irony is, of course, that the Smallweeds, with 'their stunted forms . . . their little narrow pinched ways', actually have Mr George at their mercy. Here, as elsewhere in society, frankness, generosity and strength are in danger of being corrupted or destroyed.

The scene at the pump has no relevance to the plot. It is, so to speak, an extension of George's gestures, and as such tells the reader a little more about him. George is 'a short-winded talker' by his own admission. It would be out of character for him to try to articulate the values by which he lives : any set speech from him on such a theme would be likely to sound implausible and priggish. And, although Dickens can suggest so much through posture and mannerism, these devices don't fully answer his needs in this particular case. The danger is that George will appear too wooden, too statuesque : a machine-turned ex-soldier. In the pump scene the reader glimpses the vitality and the buoyancy that inform the stance, the gestures and the measured tread.

But the passage also justifies itself in a more general way. The attitudes and energies that George expresses in a score of small movements and habits here spill over into a little aria in praise of vigour and healthy living. Numerous passages in the novels of Dickens are similar in their general effect. He has the gift of making familiar, even habitual, experiences sound freshly enjoyable – a meal, a walk, a dance, a coach ride, a boat trip, a visit to the theatre, a slide on a frozen pond. Periodically this diffused sense of the agreeableness of life is concentrated into a more extended passage of celebration. The description of Mr George at the pump celebrates the joys of a good wash.

A much lengthier exercise of this kind is the account of Tom Pinch's trip to Salisbury in *Martin Chuzzlewit*. From the point of view of plot the only relevance of the episode is the arrival of Martin Chuzzlewit Junior, but Dickens devotes several pages to a description of the city, or, rather, of Tom Pinch's reactions to the city. It is a crowded bustling description, full of lists : '. . . the thoroughfares about the market-place being filled with carts, horses, donkeys, baskets, waggons, garden-stuff, meat, tripe, pies, poultry, and huckster's wares of every opposite description . . . '. Tom explores the market, watching the farmers and inspecting the wares. He buys himself a seven-bladed pocket-knife. Later he strolls about the city, window-shopping, lingering especially at the jeweller's, the book-shops and the theatre. After attending vespers at the cathedral he is given a chance to try the organ there. His day ends at a tavern, where :

> . . . he had his little table drawn out close before the fire, and fell to work upon a well-cooked steak and smoking hot potatoes, with a strong appreciation of their excellence, and a very keen sense of enjoyment. Beside him, too, there stood a jug of most stupendous Wiltshire beer; and the effect of the whole was so transcendent, that he was obliged every now and then to lay down his knife and fork, rub his hands, and think about it.

The effect of these celebratory interludes, as of the countless incidental references to pleasurable activities or pastimes, isn't simply agreeable and enlightening. They represent an important and under-valued species of comedy. Dickens is no doubt its greatest exponent, but he is very far from being the only one. It is the comedy of the realistic school of writing – circumstantial comedy.

There has never been any difficulty in recognising and comprehending its converse, the sombre side of realism. Novelists such as Mrs Gaskell, Kingsley, Gissing, Dickens himself have shown how deprivation can destroy all happiness and hope. They convey an immediate sense of the misery of being hungry, ill-clad, cold, wet, homeless, dirty, unemployed, ignorant, sick, exhausted. Each of them implies or even asserts that such circumstantial pressures can be so strong as to make life unendurable and meaningless. Metaphysical considerations are neither here nor there : the starving man can be beyond the reach of religion, rational argument or love. Naturally the materialist's first plea is for sufficiency. Here is a hungry man – feed him; here is a sick man – tend him. Gissing makes Reardon, the impoverished New Grub Street novelist, remark : 'The difference between the man with money and the man without is simply this : the one thinks, "How shall I use my life?" and the other, "How shall I keep myself alive?" ' If Reardon had but a sufficiency, if he could cease having to worry about the very business of 'keeping himself alive', he could think and feel again; and there can be no doubt as to how he would use his regained freedom. He would read, and try to write, great works of literature; he would look to travel, to revisit Greece, to see the sun set behind Athens. True 'living' for him has to do with the life of the mind. If he had a sufficiency of food and clothing, he would virtually cease to think about such matters; he is made aware of them only by their absence. But Reardon is an unusual man, ultra-intellectual, thin-blooded, ascetic. Most of us seek, and even crave, not merely material needs but material comforts : a *pretty* dress, a *tasty* meal, a *hot* bath, a *comfortable* bed. Such comforts are vital to our sustenance in the wider sense; they contribute largely to our tacit belief that life is worth living. If 'tragedy' for the realist writer is frequently the demonstration that poverty makes many lives wretched, there is 'comedy' in the suggestion that most of us are cheered and encouraged by numerous small material pleasures.

Comedy of this kind is essential to the plays of Chekhov. In description most of them would sound lugubrious. Some characters die, some are corrupted, most are frustrated; there are sad speeches about wasted lives, thwarted hopes, gloomy prospects. Yet in the theatre *The Cherry Orchard* or *Three Sisters* should not prove dispiriting; and a major reason for the seeming paradox is the background of agreeable activities. A Sonia or an Irena may reasonably lament the apparent meaninglessness of her family's existence, but what we see of their day-to-day lives isn't, in the grain, unenjoyable. In a Chekhov play the characters are constantly doing something – playing cards, taking tea or coffee, picking flowers, reading, dozing, singing, smoking, playing the guitar. Such activities are an unspoken reminder that ordinary life, as ordinarily experienced, isn't the null joyless thing it can appear in certain moments of intensity. What keeps most of us alive and relatively cheerful is less some abstract confidence that life has meaning than a pretty concrete belief that our pleasures exceed our pains. So fundamental and widespread a belief should surely find expression in art; but since many, or most, of the pleasures concerned are trivial and diurnal they can be adequately acknowledged only in realistic art – one could almost say, despite Chekhov's example, only in fiction and the film. Perhaps the notion of circumstantial comedy hasn't been much explored because it lacks a tradition, having first been made possible by the evolution of the novel. The underlying idea, of course, has long been familiar. Just as there are passages in Dickens that could be seen as an explication of Lear's lines about the 'Poor naked wretches', so others gloss Sir Toby Belch on 'cakes and ale', or Falstaff on 'sack and sugar'. Dickens can generalise as well – 'what a Life Young Bailey's was!'; 'What larks!' – but his great art is to give substance to the generalisation through a hundred allusions and examples. In dealing with the cheerful, as with the depressing, aspects of life, the strength of the nineteenth-century novel lay in particularities; and no other novelist was as delightedly particular as Dickens.

The difficulty he faced was that of assimilating such material into his fiction, of making it contribute to the stories he told. His account of the Nubbles family's visit to the theatre in *The Old Curiosity Shop* is simply an interlude, though amiable enough in its way. It recalls his early article on Astley's. But the description of Salisbury in *Martin Chuzzlewit* clearly represents much more than the inter-polation of an unpublished Sketch by Boz. After four chapters concerned chiefly with the greed and egotism of old Martin, the Pecksniffs, Chevy Slyme and Mr Tigg, Dickens provides some relief. Salisbury is described as it appears to Tom Pinch. None of the Pecksniffs, neither of the Martin Chuzzlewits, would find such excitements in a market-day at a country town. These are the typical delights of the generous, the positive approach to life. The point is underlined by Tom's encounter with that other determined enjoyer, Mark Tapley. Tom, after all, carries innocent enthusiasm pretty far : the reader is soon to see him smacking his lips over Pecksniff's stale sandwiches and vinegary wine. Within the Pecksniff household he looks suspiciously like a sycophant, for all the extenu-ating circumstances. But Mark Tapley has much the same approach to life, and he is spry, dapper, Sam Weller-like – certainly nobody's fool. By association Tom already appears less weedy. The energy of his response to the wonders of Salisbury rehabilitates him still further. He and Mark, who between them are to re-educate young Martin, are acceptable representatives of unselfish cheerfulness.

Tom Pinch almost, but not quite, becomes a really interesting character-study. Dickens seems to be consciously trying to amend an aspect of his work that had previously been dubious. The insipidity that was presumably an unintended trait in some earlier benign characterisations is specifically made an aspect of Tom's personality. His guileless good-heartedness has an emasculating quality. He is prematurely old. The local girls look on him with affectionate pity – 'For who minded poor Mr Pinch? There was no harm in *him.*' It matters a good deal to the portrayal that the apparent lack of conventional sexual vitality is offset by an excep-tional vitality of response to sights and sounds and small pleasures. The Salisbury episode does much to establish this side of his character.

But that episode is still a relatively naïve instance of the way in which circumstantial optimism can become an essential part of the meaning of a novel by Dickens. David Copperfield's dinner-party for Traddles and the Micawbers provides a much more elaborate example; particularly the passage describing the transformation of the very unsatisfactory meat course into a highly satisfactory Devil, under the guidance of Mr Micawber :

There was a gridiron in the pantry, on which my morning rasher of bacon was cooked. We had it in, in a twinkling, and immedi-ately applied ourselves to carrying Mr Micawber's idea into effect. The division of labour to which he had referred was this : – Traddles cut the mutton into slices; Mr Micawber (who could do anything of this sort to perfection) covered them with pepper, mustard, salt, and cayenne; I put them on the gridiron, turned them with a fork, and took them off, under Mr Micawber's direction; and Mrs Micawber heated, and continually stirred, some mushroom ketchup in a little saucepan. When we had slices enough done to begin upon, we fell-to, with our sleeves still tucked up at the wrist, more slices sputtering and blazing on the fire, and our attention divided beween the mutton on our plates, and the mutton then preparing.

What with the novelty of this cookery, the excellence of it, the bustle of it, the frequent starting up to look after it, the frequent sitting down to dispose of it as the crisp slices came off the gridiron hot and hot, the being so busy, so flushed with the fire, so amused, and in the midst of such a tempting noise and savour, we reduced the leg of mutton to the bone. My own appetite came back miraculously. I am ashamed to record it, but I really believe I forgot Dora for a little while. I am satisfied that Mr and Mrs Micawber could not have enjoyed the feast more, if they had sold a bed to provide it. Traddles laughed as heartily, almost the whole time, as he ate and worked. Indeed we all did, all at once; and I dare say there never was a greater success.

Mr Micawber, the leading spirit here, has a curious role in *David Copperfield*. Lord David Cecil suggests that he is 'almost irrelevant to the action'.[16] Dr Q. D. Leavis concedes as much, but claims: 'we all feel that somehow he is a major contributor to the meaning of the book'.[17] Since he is involved in the plot only belatedly this contribution must be made through such scenes as the one quoted above. The situation itself, and Micawber's conduct and demeanour, all repay study.

The reductive view of the scene – the view I would wish to rebut – would run more or less as follows : Dickens has invented an attractive character who has nothing significant to do; this episode pleasantly displays Mr Micawber's personality, but is otherwise redundant. In fact it is closely connected, thematically, with a dozen other episodes in the novel. David's predicament concerning the dinner is far from unique. Later he and Dora invite Traddles to a still more disastrous meal, when there is no Micawber to lead a salvage operation. This particular dinner has been ruined by David's inept domestics : he is constantly at the mercy of servants and waiters, repeatedly swindled or humiliated. But here, for once, his problem finds a solution. Thanks to Mr Micawber a potentially miserable evening becomes a triumph : the meal is transformed and everyone has a good time. Micawber's character, as evinced in his speech, his letters, his clothes, is all style, and on this occasion his style is vindicated. In appearance and manner he sometimes recalls William Dorrit, Turveydrop or Skimpole; but his sense of style, unlike theirs, is more than just an expression of egotism. His initiative concerning the Devil involves optimism, resourcefulness, and also a certain wise courtesy. When he observes to David that 'accidents will occur in the best-regulated families' the remark has, of course, an ample weight of personal experience behind it; but the context underlines its validity. There is hardly a character in *David Copperfield* who has not a family secret to hide. The hard-won tolerance and resilience of Mr Micawber come to seem very desirable qualities.

At the opposite temperamental extreme is Uriah Heep – introverted where Micawber is expansive, 'umble' where he aspires to elegance, graceless where he is stylish, meanly calculating where he is feckless. Micawber's gestures are verbal and sartorial rather than physical, but in effect they are antithetical to those of Heep. The two characters are, of course, thrown into close association that leads to violent opposition, and it is in this opposition that an important aspect of the meaning of *David Copperfield* is defined.

Copperfield is manifestly in a very weak position to criticise a young man from an impoverished background who is making his way in the legal profession and aspiring to marry his employer's daughter. There are other resemblances between Heep and himself. Each is fatherless, each works hard to improve himself. As soon as David comes to live in Canterbury, Uriah sees him as a potential rival, and indeed they become, in effect, rival suitors for Agnes. Uriah's repulsiveness to David and to the reader is especially disturbing because he seems to be enacting the part allotted to David. The obvious course for Copperfield would have been to stay in Canterbury, 'come into the business' with Mr Wickfield, as Heep suggests he will, marry Agnes and write fiction in his spare time. (Such a scenario, incidentally, would reduce the novel to something like half its existing length.) The opportunities that Copperfield neglects are eagerly seized by Uriah, who strives to usurp his position in Canterbury.

Copperfield's lavish vilification of Heep is eventually justified by Heep's wickedness, but that wickedness is far from plausible. Mr Wickfield is already a hard drinker at the time of David's first meeting with him. If Uriah had only persisted in the course natural to him, the course of patience and propitiation, he would in any case have had a reasonable chance of taking over the business and winning Agnes. His obvious role was that of the Industrious Apprentice. His chicanery, his displays of power, and above all his gratuitous attempt to destroy the Strongs' marriage are out of character. If the portrayal 'works', as I think it does, it is because Dickens has induced us to see his novel not as a conventional story, but as a system of contrasts and oppositions between antithetical temperaments and life-styles, each of which holds out possibilities, temptations, opportunities to David Copperfield.

For example, if David resembles Heep in some respects, in others he relates to Micawber. They have shared poverty – Uriah is to lump them together as 'the very scum of society'. Within the Murdstone and Grinby period, for all its miseries, David on occasion shows glimpses of a Micawberesque sprightliness – notably when he goes to order himself a celebratory glass of the best ale : '. . . just draw me a glass of the Genuine Stunning, if you please, with a good head to it'. The effect of the incident is not, as the author seems to have intended, one of pathos. For once the youthful David is in control of a situation, speaking with the jauntiness of the Artful Dodger or Young Bailey. The accompanying illustration shows him poised and easy, as he leans on the counter; elsewhere he is more usually depicted perching nervously on the edge of a chair. This is David at his farthest remove from Uriah Heep, caution and self-help. Such an approach to life carries risks : presumably if David had stayed with Murdstone and Grinby he might have degenerated towards a Micawber-like fecklessness. But the Genuine Stunning scene, like the scene with the Devil, celebrates a small victory for gaiety and dash over adversity.

Micawber and Heep thus belong to the same sub-text. Heep shows how the industry, perseverance and proper deference that are proclaimed in the 'official' message of the novel can contain the seeds of envy and ugly egotism. Micawber shows how the high spirits and romantic imagination that have a lot to do with David's 'first Dissipation' and his tendency to fall in love with unsuitable girls can be agreeable and productive qualities in many circumstances. Both characterisations dramatise potentialities in David. The savagery of his rejection and denunciation of Heep is justified because he is in effect stifling meannesses within his own nature. David himself sees Mr Wickfield's weakness, suspects Annie Strong, knows that his aunt has a secret, and is destined to receive her money. It is in his power to do most of the damage that Heep does.

The contrast is developed further, and to different effect, in the characters of Traddles and Steerforth. Heep threatens harm to most of the people David loves : Betsey Trotwood, the Wickfields, the Strongs, the Micawbers. But thanks to Traddles, and in particular to Micawber himself, he is thwarted. Steerforth, being young, handsome and well-to-do, stands much more obviously than Micawber for style, for charm; and he does more than threaten – he actually destroys David's childhood haven, the home of the Peggottys. Like

Heep he seems almost to act on David's behalf, in that he seduces the girl whom David himself loves, or has loved. If the dangerousness or potential ugliness of Micawber's mode of life is not particularly stressed, it is because the point is amply made in the story of Steerforth and the Peggottys. The wickedness and the physical nastiness of Heep have to be grotesquely magnified to make them an adequate counterpoise to the destruction wrought by Steerforth. Traddles represents the good qualities that Uriah perverts, being hard-working, patient and unassuming. He is brave enough to denounce Steerforth at school, and wise enough to help Micawber outwit Heep. Copperfield's violent antipathy to Heep and passionate attachment to Steerforth are cancelled by events; and he is left with a proper appreciation of the complementary virtues of Traddles and Micawber.

My account of the connections between these five characters touches on only one of the themes of *David Copperfield*, though I take it to be a major one. And for the sake of clarity I have deliberately simplified and been schematic. But clearly, I think, the novel works in some such way as I have described. The reappearance of Micawber, Traddles, Steerforth, Miss Murdstone and the Peggottys brings David's childhood into relationship with his adulthood. He has to reconcile a variety of experiences, affections, examples, loyalties, duties, possible life-styles. One sub-plot balances and modifies another. But for his later encounters with Micawber, David's period with Murdstone and Grinby might seem to have left no impression on his character. But for Micawber's defeat of Uriah Heep, Steerforth's seduction of Emily might imply a denunciation of charm. But for Uriah's repulsiveness and treacheries, the novel could appear to present too simple-minded an advertisement for diligence, early rising and the determined pursuit of decent ambition.

If the novel is seen in this light, not as a collection of stories but as a system of contrasting modes of living, contrasting kinds of energy, then Dickens's interest in posture, gesture, habits of speech or dress must be acknowledged to be central to his purpose. In a conventional novel such detail commonly serves merely to presage or to confirm the characteristics displayed in more significant actions. In *David Copperfield* it provides the essential statement : Heep's essential nastiness is implicit in his clammy handshake, and Micawber's essential good nature in the way he makes punch.

How far the effects I've been describing were intended by the author I don't know. One of the intriguing things about *David Copperfield* is that its hidden patterns of correspondence, unlike those of Dickens's later novels, are significantly at variance with its ostensible themes. The author's mastery of externalities makes it possible for him to say more than he consciously realises. When reading a Dickens novel one should trust the narration rather than the narrator.

Chapter 4

Clothes and Accoutrements

'Madam,' said *Adams*, 'if it be not impertinent, I should be glad
to know how this Gentleman was drest.'

Henry Fielding, *Joseph Andrews*

He wore a short jacket of brown corduroy, newer than the
remainder of his suit, which was a fustian waistcoat with white
horn buttons, breeches of the same, tanned leggings, and a straw
hat overlaid with black glazed canvas.

Thomas Hardy, *The Mayor of Casterbridge*

Poll wore in his sporting character, a velveteen coat, a great deal
of blue stocking, ankle boots, a neckerchief of some bright colour,
and a very tall hat. Pursuing his more quiet occupation of barber,
he generally subsided into an apron not over-clean, a flannel
jacket, and corduroy knee-shorts.

Charles Dickens, *Martin Chuzzlewit*

In the social classification of the nether world . . . it will be
convenient to distinguish broadly, and with reference to males
alone, the two great sections of those who do, and those who do
not, wear collars. Each of these orders would, it is obvious, offer
much scope to an analyst delighting in subtle gradation. Taking
the collarless, how shrewdly might one discriminate between the
many kinds of neckcloth which our climate renders necessary as a
substitute for the nobler article of attire! The navvy, the
scaffolder, the costermonger, the cab-tout – innumerable would be
the varieties of texture, of fold, of knot, observed in the ranks of
unskilled labour. And among those whose higher station is
indicated by the linen or paper symbol, what a gap between the
mechanic with collar attached to a flannel shirt, and just visible
along the top of a black tie, and the shopman whose pride it is to
adorn himself with the very ugliest neck-encloser put in vogue by
aristocratic sanction.

George Gissing, *The Nether World*

Irishmen both! You might know them, if they were masked, by their long-tailed blue coats and bright buttons, and their drab trousers, which they wear like men well used to working dresses, who are easy in no others.

Charles Dickens, *American Notes*

6. *Possessional Territory*: Any set of objects that can be identified with the self and arrayed around the body wherever it is. The central examples are spoken of as 'personal effects' – easily detachable possessions such as jackets, hats, gloves, cigarette packs, matches, handbags and what they contain, and parcels.

Erving Goffman, *Relations in Public*

'There's no such thing as an isolated man or woman; we're each of us made up of some cluster of appurtenances. What shall we call our "self"? Where does it begin? where does it end? It over-flows into everything that belongs to us – and then it flows back again. I know a large part of myself is in the clothes I choose to wear. I've a great respect for *things*! One's self – for other people – is one's expression of one's self; and one's house, one's furniture, one's garments, the books one reads, the company one keeps – these things are all expressive.'

Henry James, *The Portrait of a Lady*

For there can be hardly anything less connected with a woman's personality than drapery which she has neither designed, manu-factured, cut, sewed, nor even seen, except by a glance of approval when told that such and such a shape and colour must be had because it has been decided by others as imperative at that particular time.

Thomas Hardy, *The Woodlanders*

What new articles she bought for herself, were all such as would make a show, and an impression upon the ladies of Hollingford. She argued with herself that linen, and all underclothing, would never be seen; while she knew that every gown she had, would give rise to much discussion, and would be counted up in the little town.

So her stock of underclothing was very small, and scarcely any of it new; but it was made of dainty material, and was finely mended up by her deft fingers, many a night long after her pupils were in bed. . . .

Elizabeth Gaskell, *Wives and Daughters*

If she had only a dress to wear in the afternoons! The old yellow thing on her back would never do. But one of her cotton prints was pretty fresh; she must get a bit of red ribbon – that would

D

make a difference. She had heard that the housemaids in places like Woodview always changed their dresses twice a day, and on Sundays went out in silk mantles and hats in the newest fashion. As for the lady's-maid, she of course had all her mistress's clothes, and walked with the butler.

George Moore, Esther Waters

'Tell J'mima to put on her white muslin, Tilly,' screamed Mrs Ivins, with motherly anxiety; and down came J'mima herself soon afterwards in a white muslin gown carefully hooked and eyed, and little red shawl, plentifully pinned, and white straw bonnet trimmed with red ribbons, and a small necklace, and large pair of bracelets, and Denmark satin shoes, and open-worked stockings, white cotton gloves on her fingers, and a cambric pocket-handkerchief, carefully folded up, in her hand – all quite genteel and ladylike.

Charles Dickens, Sketches by Boz

A great white cap, with a quantity of opaque frilling that was always flapping about, apologised for Maggy's baldness, and made it so very difficult for her old black bonnet to retain its place upon her head, that it held on round her neck like a gipsy's baby. A commission of haberdashers could alone have reported what the rest of her poor dress was made of; but it had a strong general resemblance to seaweed, with here and there a gigantic tea-leaf. Her shawl looked particularly like a tea-leaf, after long infusion.

Charles Dickens, Little Dorrit

Moreover, I respected the fellow. Yes; I respected his collars, his vast cuffs, his brushed hair. His appearance was certainly that of a hairdresser's dummy; but in the great demoralisation of the land he kept up his appearance. That's backbone. His starched collars and got-up shirt-fronts were achievements of character.

Joseph Conrad, Heart of Darkness

The shabbiness of these attendants upon shabbiness, the poverty of these insolvent waiters upon insolvency, was a sight to see. Such threadbare coats and trousers, such fusty gowns and shawls, such squashed hats and bonnets, such boots and shoes, such umbrellas and walking-sticks, never were seen in Rag Fair. All of them wore the cast-off clothes of other men and women; were made up of patches and pieces of other people's individuality, and had no sartorial existence of their own proper.

Charles Dickens, Little Dorrit

What an excellent example of the power of dress, young Oliver Twist was! Wrapped in the blanket which had hitherto formed his only covering, he might have been the child of a nobleman or a beggar; it would have been hard for the haughtiest stranger to have assigned him his proper station in society. But now that he was enveloped in the old calico robes which had grown yellow in the same service, he was badged and ticketed, and fell into his place at once – a parish child – the orphan of a workhouse – the humble, half-starved drudge – to be cuffed and buffeted through the world – despised by all, and pitied by none.

Charles Dickens, Oliver Twist

A very stout, puffy man, in buckskins and Hessian boots, with several immense neckcloths, that rose almost to his nose, with a red-striped waistcoat and an apple-green coat with steel buttons almost as large as crown pieces (it was the morning costume of a dandy or blood of those days), was reading the paper by the fire. . . .

W. M. Thackeray, Vanity Fair

He is a county Member, and has been from time whereof the memory of man is not to the contrary. Look at his loose, wide, brown coat, with capacious pockets on each side; the knee-breeches and boots, the immensely long waistcoat, and silver watch-chain dangling below it, the wide-brimmed brown hat, and the white handkerchief tied in a great bow, with straggling ends sticking out beyond his shirt-frill. It is a costume one seldom sees nowadays, and when the few who wear it have died off, it will be quite extinct.

Charles Dickens, Sketches by Boz

A complete change in my dress was imperatively necessary for many reasons. I took off my silk gown to begin with, because the slightest noise from it on that still night might have betrayed me. I next removed the white and cumbersome parts of my under-clothing, and replaced them by a petticoat of dark flannel. Over this I put my black travelling cloak, and pulled the hood on to my head. In my ordinary evening costume I took up the room of three men at least. In my present dress, when it was held close about me, no man could have passed through the narrowest spaces more easily than I.

Wilkie Collins, The Woman in White

There, between the cider-mug and the candle, stood this interesting receptacle of the little unknown's foot; and a very pretty boot it was. A character, in fact – the flexible bend at the instep, the rounded localities of the small nestling toes, scratches from careless scampers now forgotten – all, as repeated in the tell-tale leather, evidencing a nature and a bias. Dick surveyed it with a delicate feeling that he had no right to do so without having first asked the owner of the foot's permission.

Thomas Hardy, *Under the Greenwood Tree*

'That the man was highly intellectual is of course obvious upon the face of it, and also that he was fairly well-to-do within the last three years, although he has now fallen upon evil days. He had foresight, but has less now than formerly, pointing to a moral retrogression, which, when taken with the decline of his fortunes, seems to indicate some evil influence, probably drink, at work upon him. This may account also for the obvious fact that his wife has ceased to love him. . . .

'He has, however, retained some degree of self-respect. . . . He is a man who leads a sedentary life, goes out little, is out of training entirely, is middle-aged, has grizzled hair which he has had cut within the last few days, and which he anoints with lime-cream. These are the more patent facts which are to be deduced from his hat.'

A. Conan Doyle, *The Adventures of Sherlock Holmes*

'Cos that there's the wale, the bonnet, and the gownd. It is her and it an't her. It an't her hand, nor yet her rings, nor yet her woice. But that there's the wale, the bonnet, and the gownd, and they're wore the same way wot she wore 'em, and it's her height wot she wos, and she giv me a sov'ring and hooked it.'

Charles Dickens, *Bleak House*

I

Hardy seems to show us Tess Durbeyfield's entire wardrobe. We see her wearing, for example, her best dress of white muslin, a pink cotton working-jacket, 'a gray serge cape, a red woollen cravat, a stuff skirt covered by a whitey-brown wrapper, and buff-leather gloves', 'a soft gray woollen gown, with white crape quilling . . . and a black velvet jacket and hat', and 'a cashmere dressing-gown of gray-white'. The diversity is appropriate to the author's effort to show his heroine in a wide variety of moods and circumstances. Although few nineteenth-century English novelists go into anything like such detail, most of them choose to comment on what their characters wear. It's certainly evident that they seem automatically and invariably to conceive of them as fully clad, equipped for social action. Hardy's very physical portrayal of Tess is quite exceptional. Normally bodies are kept out of sight and out of consideration. Mr

George is lucky to get even as far as a pump bare-chested. Marian Halcombe and Elfride Swancourt show a truly uncommon pluck and resourcefulness when they strip off some of their numerous garments to cope with an emergency.

At first glance detailed descriptions of clothes, however relevant to the visual life of a novel, might seem to promise little psychological or even social information. The more obvious indications can usually be summed up in a single adjective or adverb : 'wearing a shabby suit'; 'fashionably dressed'. Subtler inferences are likely to be dubious, since people of very different temperaments may chance to choose similar outfits. There is nothing to prevent Uriah Heep from patronising Mr Wickfield's tailor. The information that one reads in a face may be deceptive, but it is directly personal and also fairly stable. Faces alter only over a period of months or even years; while a Victorian lady might change her dress several times a day. (It is because men changed less frequently, I take it, that the novelists of the period were more inclined to describe male than female attire.) Face and gesture say more than clothes, in the majority of cases, and are therefore better worth depicting.

But it must be remembered that through much of the nineteenth century it was quite possible that one might see nothing, technically, of a person to whom one was introduced save the area between collar and hat. It was natural to seek meanings in the fabrics that hid the rest of the organism. In any case dress was much more expressive than it has since become, because there was more of it, and it was much more formalised. We have largely done away with galoshes, gloves, hats, waistcoats, boas, shawls, parasols, muffs and walking-sticks. Leonard Bast's anxiety about his umbrella is in danger of looking obsessive and valetudinarian. Many species and sub-species of working-dress have disappeared. Class differences are infinitely less visible – denim has been a great leveller. Mourning is very little in evidence. Even fashion itself is out of fashion : people wear pretty much what they please. Because we wouldn't expect clothes to tell us much nowadays, it is easy for us to read unthinkingly through a Victorian description that in its own time carefully placed a character as dandified, frumpish, lower middle-class, old-fashioned, artistic or pretentious. Yesterday's gestures and facial expressions can still speak to us pretty directly, but yesterday's garments cannot. The student must learn to construe them.

In the novels of Dickens clothing is often an extension of gesture, similarly conveying a sense of style. Just as Jaggers throws his great forefinger to menacing effect, so he can threaten by creaking his boots, or even by making play with a handkerchief :

He always carried (I have not yet mentioned it, I think) a pocket-handkerchief of rich silk and of imposing proportions, which was of great value to him in his profession. I have seen him so terrify a client or a witness by ceremoniously unfolding this pocket-handkerchief as if he were immediately going to blow his nose, and then pausing, as if he knew he should not have time to do it, before such client or witness committed himself, that the self-committal has followed directly, quite as a matter of course.

Jaggers's handkerchief, like the Artful Dodger's precarious hat, exists to provide an occasion for gesture. Dick Swiveller's cane is a flourish in itself, 'having at the top a bone hand with the semblance of a ring on its little finger and a black ball in its grasp'. It goes with his brass buttons, bright neckerchief and a romantic turn of speech.

In Dickens's most developed character-portrayals the information concerning clothes and accoutrements does not merely confirm the suggestions implicit in his account of face or gesture, but carries them farther. His introduction of Miss Tox in *Dombey and Son* provides a conveniently compact example of the method. Miss Tox's countenance is focused round her 'stupendously aquiline' nose, with its 'little knob in the very centre or key-stone of the bridge, whence it tended downwards towards her face . . .'. She has a manner, an attentive, propitiatory manner, and gestures to match it : 'Her hands had contracted a spasmodic habit of raising themselves of their own accord as in involuntary admiration.' But, in this first account of Miss Tox, Dickens makes her clothes tell most of the story :

Miss Tox's dress, though perfectly genteel and good, had a certain character of angularity and scantiness. She was accustomed to wear odd weedy little flowers in her bonnets and caps. Strange grasses were sometimes perceived in her hair; and it was observed by the curious, of all her collars, frills, tuckers, wristbands, and other gossamer articles – indeed of everything she wore which had two ends to it intended to unite – that the two ends were never on good terms, and wouldn't quite meet without a struggle. She had furry articles for winter wear, as tippets, boas, and muffs, which stood up on end in a rampant manner, and were not at all sleek. She was much given to the carrying about of small bags with snaps to them, that went off like little pistols when they were shut up; and when full-dressed, she wore round her neck the barrenest of lockets, representing a fishy old eye, with no approach to speculation in it.

Although the explicit point Dickens proceeds to make is that Miss Tox appears to be 'a lady of what is called limited independence', his description has conveyed a good deal more than that. Of course her collars and wristbands imply that she can't make ends meet in the conventional sense, but they also suggest a failed attempt to look attractively feminine. The flowers and grasses hint at romantic aspirations of a hopeless kind. Like her own nose Miss Tox achieves gentility, but not beauty. Her adornments fail to adorn; her wish to please exceeds her capacities. The barren fishy locket, the small bags that snap shut, the 'mincing gait' that Dickens later mentions combine with her 'faded air' to bespeak an imposed habit of old maidenliness. Each of the separate details Dickens includes says something about Miss Tox, but the ensemble is much more than the sum total of these parts.

I took these examples from Dickens because he seems to have been particularly aware of the complex effects that descriptions of dress could achieve. The simpler purposes – allaying the reader's curiosity, vivifying a scene, loosely defining a new character – are by no means unimportant, but they hardly require elucidation. Most of the novelists of the period attempted occasionally what Dickens attempted repeatedly : to make clothes or accoutrements psychologically revealing. The possibilities of the technique, as I hope later to show, go well beyond what is suggested by the full, but fairly straightforward, portrayal of Miss Tox. But there is a preliminary difficulty of a curious kind. Because these properties are strictly speaking external to their owner, strong emphasis on them can actually deflect attention away from the character concerned. If clothes are described too minutely or emphatically the person inside them can disappear. In the next two sections I will consider two contrasting kinds of miscalculation.

II

The historical novelist is particularly given to describing clothes. Reasonably enough he wants to ensure that his characters will be appropriately visualised by the reader. But the attempt calls for considerable tact. Here is an extract from Kingsley's introduction of Hypatia :

> For in the light arm-chair . . . sat a woman, of some five-and-twenty years . . . dressed . . . in a simple old snow-white Ionic robe, falling to the feet and reaching to the throat, and of that peculiarly severe and graceful fashion in which the upper part of

the dress falls downward again from the neck to the waist in a sort of cape, entirely hiding the outline of the bust, while it leaves the arms and the point of the shoulders bare. Her dress was entirely without ornament, except the two narrow purple stripes down the front, which marked her rank as a Roman citizen, the gold-embroidered shoes upon her feet, and the gold net, which looped back, from her forehead to her neck, hair the colour and gloss of which were hardly distinguishable from that of the metal itself. . . .

Like parts of *Romola*, the passage owes too much to research. The author's concern to get all the details of costume correct so obviously takes precedence, for the moment, over any narrative interest that the novel begins to read like a fictionalised history lesson. Hypatia is presented not as she will be seen by her father – the next person to enter the room – but as she would have appeared to Kingsley's readers, to whom her costume would have been unfamiliar. Instead of the reader being transported to the fifth century, Hypatia is brought into the nineteenth.

At the opposite extreme is a curious speech from that curious work, *The Dynasts*. Some ladies of Brussels are watching the columns of British soldiers march out of the city, and a Gentleman Opposite provides a commentary for them :

The foot coming up now are the Seventy-ninth. (*They pass.*) . . . These next are the Ninety-fifth. (*They pass.*) . . . These are the First Foot-guards. (*They pass, playing 'British Grenadiers'.*) . . . The Fusileer-guards now. (*They pass.*) . . . Now the Coldstreamers. (*They pass. He looks up towards the Parc.*) Several Hanoverian regiments under Colonel Best are coming next. (*They pass, with their bands and colours. An interval.*)

Hardy announces in his Preface that '*The Dynasts* is intended simply for mental performance, and not for the stage'. He surely shows an extraordinary confidence in the resources of the theatre of the mind. Without descriptive aid of any kind the reader is asked to picture a dozen different regiments (the quotation above is only an extract from the commentary) and to hear the relevant band-music. Only a military historian with a powerful imagination, a musical ear and time on his hands could hope to experience the scene as the author seems to have meant it to be experienced.

But even the lay reader, who couldn't tell the Ninety-seventh from the Seventy-ninth, is unlikely to find that the scene leaves his imagination completely blank. We all carry recollections of military parades and march-pasts, of course, but there's more to the matter than that. For most of us such conception as we have of different historical periods is to a great extent based on notions of what people used to wear at the relevant time – notions derived from portraits, prints, museums, and historical plays and films. Military parades give pleasure partly because the dress-uniforms seem to bring history to life : the marching troops look like animated toy soldiers. When we read a historical novel our very generalised ideas about costume form part of our imaginative response. We expect – perhaps even demand – that the writer will rouse them and nourish them.

This situation is by no means an unmixed blessing from the novelist's point of view, because the generalised ideas are equivocal. Certainly they involve an attempt to envisage a past reality – did the ladies *really* wear such dresses? did the soldiers *really* fight in such uniforms? But at the same time they incorporate an element of unreality. The costumes of the past are pretty, picturesque, quaint. It is hard to take them or their wearers seriously, hard to imagine that a Hussar or a Dragoon could bleed to death from a sword wound. The more we relish the clothes, the less we respond to the people inside them. It's not surprising that 'costume drama' should have become a pejorative term. An actor condemned to play the part of Napoleon Bonaparte has only to don the familiar uniform and hat and slip one hand into his breast, to be reduced to a walking waxwork. For the same sort of reason the historical novelist is likely to decline into a Madame Tussaud.

Hardy himself, in *The Trumpet-Major*, shows an interesting way of tackling the problem. He meets it head-on. The first words of the novel are : 'In the days of high-waisted and muslin-gowned women. . . .' This is to be unashamedly a costume piece. Within a page or two the soldiers are arriving, resplendently uniformed : '. . . white buckskin pantaloons, three-quarter boots, scarlet shakos set off with lace, mustachios waxed to a needle point; and above all, those richly ornamented blue jackets mantled with the historic pelisse – that fascination to women, and encumbrance to the wearers themselves'. Hardy describes with comparable lavishness the clothes of the ladies – of the soldiers' 'butterfly wives', of Mrs Garland on her wedding-day, of Matilda Johnson, of Anne herself : 'Anne wore her celebrated celestial blue pelisse, her Leghorn hat, and her muslin dress with the waist under the arms; the latter being decorated with excellent Honiton lace. . . .'

When Anne goes to Budmouth to see the King and his entourage, she feels that she is 'close to and looking into the stream of recorded history, within whose banks the littlest things are great, and outside which she and the general bulk of the human race were content to live on as an unreckoned, unheeded superfluity'. But when these ordinary people look at the notabilities, what they see is clothes : ' "Now you can see his feather!" "There's her hat!" "There's her Majesty's India muslin shawl!" ' Captain Hardy appears as 'a hale man in the prime of life, wearing a blue uniform, gilt epaulettes, cocked hat, and sword . . .'.

It isn't Hardy's purpose to contrast the remoteness of the famous figures with the individuality of his leading characters, for Anne, John and Bob have only a very limited psychological life. This is a folk-tale. The pretty heroine has to choose between Gallant Soldier and Fickle Sailor. It is John's uniform that woos her : 'So his epaulettes and blue jacket, and Anne's yellow gipsy hat, were often seen in different parts of the garden at the same time. . . . By degrees his gold lace, buckles, and spurs lost all their strangeness and were as familiar to her as her own clothes.' Bob eventually recaptures Anne's attention by parading up and down that same garden in his brand-new naval officer's uniform.

Of course this emphasis on the clothes of the characters diminishes their individuality. Hardy is making that very point. He comments, when he is describing the military review :

> The spectators, who, unlike our party, had no personal interest in the soldiery, saw only troops and battalions in the concrete, straight lines of red, straight lines of blue, white lines formed of innumerable knee-breeches, black lines formed of many gaiters, coming and going in kaleidoscopic change. Who thought of every point in the line as an isolated man, each dwelling all to himself in the hermitage of his own mind?

In nearly all Hardy's novels he is concerned to dramatise both the precious uniqueness of the individual life and its microscopic insignificance in larger contexts of space or time. *The Trumpet-Major* is a gentle book, because the passage of time has softened that contrast. Just as the 'subtle mist of superfine flour from the grinding-room' creeps into the Garlands' dwelling, 'quite invisible, but making its presence known in the course of time by giving a pallid and ghostly look to the best furniture', so intervening minutes, hours and days mollify and tranquillise our apprehension of past joys and sorrows. Hardy looks back on the doings at Overcombe Mill 'through the mists' of seventy or eighty years. John Loveday, the better man, loses Anne Garland to his brother and is doomed to die in Spain. But by the time Hardy tells the story Anne, Bob and all the other characters are also dead; their rivalries have been reconciled. *The Trumpet-Major* is usually accounted a minor novel, because it sacrifices psychological interest to picturesqueness and charm; but it seems to me a remarkable achievement of its kind. Hardy has found a means of transforming the characteristic weakness of historical fiction into a strength. His subject is not so much the past as the way in which we view the past.

III

Clothes will often be uninformative, since many people are concerned only to achieve a certain reasonable standard of comfort and neatness. But the clothes of the very poor must be significant to them as a constant source of misery and struggle. Dickens knows this very well. It is a bitter moment for Oliver Twist when he has to put on once more the 'sad rags' that he had discarded at Mr Brownlow's, 'delighted to think that they were safely gone, and that there was now no possible danger of his ever being able to wear them again'. But many of Dickens's impoverished characters contrive to carry their shabbiness jauntily. Even Maggy is picturesque in her way. Where Dickens does try to suggest the discomfort that worn clothing can cause he is usually unspecific. By contrast Gissing is a novelist who is at pains to show as precisely as possible what old clothes look like, thereby to demonstrate more feelingly what they can do to the wearer. Here, from *New Grub Street*, is his description of Mr Quarmby's apparel :

> His garb must have seen a great deal of Museum service; it consisted of a jacket, something between brown and blue, hanging in capacious shapelessness, a waistcoat half open for lack of buttons and with one of the pockets coming unsewn, a pair of bronze-hued trousers which had all run to knee. Necktie he had none, and his linen made distinct appeal to the laundress.

It is quite a full account, but has no 'entertainment' value whatever. Mr Quarmby's appearance is quite devoid of style; it is neither picturesque nor amusing. His clothing looks ugly and uncomfortable, and suggests an ugly and uncomfortable mode of existence. The reference to his linen is not incidental : Gissing does not baulk at dirt. Later in the novel he attacks at some length the comfortable view 'that cleanliness is a luxury within reach even of the poorest'.

A sense of encroaching physical squalor helps persuade Amy
Reardon to desert her husband :

> No, no; cleanliness is a costly thing, and a troublesome thing
> when appliances and means have to be improvised. It was, in
> part, the understanding she had gained of this side of the life of
> poverty that made Amy shrink in dread from the still narrower
> lodgings to which Reardon invited her. She knew how subtly
> one's self-respect can be undermined by sordid conditions.

Seen from this point of view – and it is a point of view that Gissing
adopts again and again – Quarmby's clothes reveal a good deal
about his mental and spiritual morale.

Through Biffen, a still poorer denizen of New Grub Street, whose
entire outfit 'would perhaps have sold for three-and-sixpence at an
old clothes dealer's', Gissing dramatises another of the difficulties
involved in keeping up appearances. When he is visiting Reardon,
Biffen resolutely declines to remove his overcoat. His friend does
not press the matter, rightly inferring that he wishes to hide the
fact that his jacket is at the pawnbroker's. Because he lives for his
writing Biffen can endure such embarrassments with tolerable
stoicism. Hood, in *A Life's Morning*, is less fortunate. His hat is
blown away while he is on a train journey towards Hebsworth,
where he is to deliver a message for his employer. The only money
he has with him is a ten-pound note belonging to that employer;
but 'it was impossible to go through Hebsworth with uncovered
head, or to present himself hatless at the office of Legge Brothers'.
This dilemma, which today seems as grotesque as it is pitiful, proves
to be literally fatal. When Hood's train arrives he hires a cab, in
sheer panic, and makes for the nearest hatter's :

> The agony of embarrassment has driven shy men to strange
> audacities, but who ever dared more than this? *He would be
> compelled to change the note*!

Hood's action leads directly to his dismissal and to suicide.

The chapter in which the incident on the train is described is
called 'Circumstance'. The people Gissing usually elects to write
about are poor enough to find their clothing a circumstance of
determining importance. In *New Grub Street* Biffen talks of the
possibilities of a literature that would deal with the daily life 'of
that vast majority of people who are at the mercy of paltry circumstance'. He instances 'poor Allen, who lost the most valuable oppor-

tunity of his life because he hadn't a clean shirt to put on . . .'. The
main plot of *New Grub Street* itself takes in an episode of just that
kind. When Reardon goes to visit his estranged wife there is a real
chance of reconciliation. The stumbling-block proves to be his
clothes :

> His soft felt hat, never brushed for months, was a greyish green,
> and stained round the band with perspiration. His necktie was
> discoloured and worn. Coat and waistcoat might pass muster, but
> of the trousers the less said the better. One of his boots was
> patched, and both were all but heelless.
>
> Very well; let her see him thus. Let her understand what it
> meant to live on twelve and sixpence a week.
>
> Though it was cold and wet he could not put on his overcoat.
> Three years ago it had been a fairly good ulster; at present, the
> edges of the sleeves were frayed, two buttons were missing, and
> the original hue of the cloth was indeterminable.

When he arrives, after a six-mile walk through wind and rain, the
meeting proves hopeless from the start. For Amy the worn wet suit
and the 'muddy and shapeless boots' symbolise the disgrace of
economic and social decline. She cannot bring herself even to shake
hands with Reardon. Intellectually she knows that his shabbiness is
inevitable and excusable, but after five months of living among
well-dressed people she is unable to stifle an instinctive feeling of
class difference. Her husband senses her coolness and responds in
kind. Reserve hardens into hostility on both sides, and the breach
becomes absolute. Early in the encounter Gissing draws the
Biffenesque moral : 'Had Reardon been practical man enough to
procure by hook or by crook a decent suit of clothes for this interview, that ridiculous trifle might have made all the difference in
what was to result.'

Reardon gets soaked again on his gloomy journey home, and one
of his boots lets water. In a day or two he is bed-ridden with a
heavy cold. From that time forward his health deteriorates with
some rapidity until he dies from inflammation of the lungs. His
dilapidated clothes have cost him more than his marriage.

In another novelist this might seem glib; and perhaps Gissing
himself is open to the criticism. With reasonable luck one shouldn't
find that wet feet lead to inflammation of the lungs. But Gissing's
main characters don't have reasonable luck, as it were by definition,
because they come from the ranks of the intelligent poor. The
author repeatedly makes the point that any poor man is physically

at risk, being inadequately clothed and fed, and unable to afford proper medical treatment. But the intelligent poor man is yet worse off, in that he is sensitively aware of the mental and spiritual degradation that poverty can cause. Gradually his morale fails, and he loses some of his will to live. As his clothes wear out, so his body and soul begin to wear out. Gissing is the most dyspeptic of novelists : all his right-thinking characters are liable to serious illness. In his view Reardon's fate would be more or less inevitable, because he has nothing left to live for.

Given his scepticism about the feasibility, or even the desirability, of political remedies, Gissing's economic determinism – for that is what it amounts to – is extremely dispiriting. It has a confining, and even a diminishing, effect on his work, because it belittles the characters. Gissing makes it apparent that there is nothing that Reardon could say or do, granted the shabbiness of his clothes, which could materially influence his wife. Accordingly he describes these clothes far more fully than he ever describes Reardon's face. The reader's sympathy is likely to be keen, but a little dismissive. One can take only a restricted *kind* of interest in a character whose face is less vivid than his hat, and whose fate is so entirely at the mercy of his boots.

IV

Clothes can most obviously be of psychological interest as an expression of an individual style. A man dresses up as himself, or as the person he would like to be. Hardy's account of Fancy Day's boot is a reminder that we also leave our imprint on our clothes in a literal sense. Our garments adapt themselves to the curves and angularities and habitual movements of our bodies. Over a period of time they can acquire a biographical interest, as Dickens was already aware when he wrote *Sketches by Boz*. In 'Meditations in Monmouth Street' he examines a boy's suit in a second-hand clothes shop :

> It had belonged to a town boy, we could see; there was a shortness about the legs and arms of the suit; and a bagging at the knees, peculiar to the rising youth of London streets. A small day-school he had been at, evidently. If it had been a regular boys' school they wouldn't have let him play on the floor so much, and rub his knees so white. He had an indulgent mother too, and plenty of halfpence, as the numerous smears of some sticky substance about the pockets, and just below the chin, which even the salesman's

skill could not succeed in disguising, sufficiently betokened. They were decent people, but not overburdened with riches, or he would not have so far outgrown the suit when he passed into those corduroys with the round jacket; in which he went to a boys' school, however, and learnt to write – and in ink of pretty tolerable blackness too, if the place where he used to wipe his pen might be taken as evidence.

This sketch should have seemed much more remarkable when it first appeared than it does today. What previous writer had looked at clothes with even remotely similar attentiveness? But, then, what novelist would have had cause to do so? – for the poor had played very little part in fiction, and it was only the poor who would be likely to keep their garments long enough to wear a life-style into them. As our first writer of fiction to *see* the working class Dickens automatically had a new technique at his disposal. But the extract from 'Monmouth Street' does suggest a problem. The novel offers limited scope for the detailed analysis of specimen garments. Even Sherlock Holmes is allowed only the occasional set-piece with walking-stick or hat. Dick Dewy feels a positive twinge of embarrassment at seeing Fancy's boot far away from its owner's foot. The acuteness of observation that Boz displays will need to be adjusted to the dynamic situations that narrative normally requires.

The power of clothes to convey a sense of style would seem to have been greatly restricted by the formalities of the Victorian period. In the novels of Dickens it is usually the poor who are interestingly inventive or eccentric in their garb : the well-to-do tend merely to dress respectably. If Miss Tox's income were doubled her personality might remain unchanged, but it would be expressed less obviously in her costume. There is some idiosyncrasy of dress, of course, even among Dickens's more prosperous characters. A number of the men, especially, go in for old-fashioned clothes : a list of those who wear knee-breeches would be quite extensive. Betsey Trotwood's semi-masculine attire expresses the personality she has defensively assumed. Miss Havisham's yellowish wedding-outfit might seem too heavily symbolic to be psychologically interesting or even plausible; but Dickens just about gets away with it through skilful stylisation, and because the symbolism can be seen as Miss Havisham's rather than his own. Mrs Jellyby's attire is unorthodox in its negligence : she is too preoccupied with Africa to think about it. That of Mr Turveydrop, her polar opposite, is unorthodox in its elaboration : he thinks about nothing else.

But more generally Dickens's technique with his 'respectable' characters is not to make their clothing freakish, but to give it a limited individuality that is metaphorically appropriate. Here is part of the introductory description of Mr Tulkinghorn in *Bleak House* :

> He is of what is called the old school – a phrase generally meaning any school that seems never to have been young – and wears knee breeches tied with ribbons, and gaiters or stockings. One peculiarity of his black clothes, and of his black stockings, be they silk or worsted, is, that they never shine. Mute, close, irresponsive to any glancing light, his dress is like himself. He never converses, when not professionally consulted.

Tulkinghorn is another old-fangled dresser : as the parenthesis implies, he is years removed from youthful passions, if ever he had any. But the more important point comes later – that his clothes are 'mute, close, irresponsive' as he himself is. Technically Mr Tulkinghorn presents a problem. He is a mysterious man, without family or friends. His motives are obscure. Unless his duties require him to speak he prefers to remain silent. He has no face to speak of : effectively his physical presence consists of a pair of spectacles and his clothes. Much of his time is spent hovering wordlessly in the houses of the great. How can such a man have fictional substance? Dickens makes two points at once, by giving him some visual life in the form of his rusty old-fashioned clothes (of which the reader is to be regularly reminded), and by causing those clothes to imply his secretiveness and taciturnity. On Tulkinghorn's subsequent appearances a reference to his breeches becomes a reference to his personality. The pattern of metaphor is soon extended. His apartment, we are told, is 'like as he is to look at' : 'Rusty, out of date, withdrawing from attention, able to afford it.' His great treat is a bottle of his own port, fifty years old, that has to be brought up from the 'silence and seclusion' of his remote cellars. Merely to obtain it is an arcane ritual : '. . . Mr Tulkinghorn takes a small key from his pocket, unlocks a drawer in which there is another key, which unlocks a chest in which there is another key, and so comes to the cellar-key, with which he prepares to descend to the regions of old wine'. Everything about Mr Tulkinghorn is made to speak for him, since he declines to speak for himself.

The meaningfulness of his clothes is to be understood from Dickens's descriptions of them, rather than being implicit in the garments themselves. Mr Vholes, another solicitor in *Bleak House*, also chooses to dress himself in black; but in his case the associations are different. He 'lifts off his tight hat as if he were scalping himself', shakes hands with a black glove that seems to contain no fingers. Eventually he is to destroy his client, Richard Carstone. His black garb identifies him as an agent of death.

In summary, either of these portrayals, or both, may sound facile. If I were trying to make out a case for Dickens as a 'symbolic' writer I would certainly find these descriptions too obvious to be worth quoting. The skill I am trying to illustrate here is of a rather different kind. In most nineteenth-century novels, even in most of the great nineteenth-century novels, a character with the relatively minor status of a Tulkinghorn or a Vholes would have neither visual nor psychological life. Information about his clothes, or his home, of his port, or his pimples would not be included because it would seem to be mere redundancy. But in *Bleak House* Dickens everywhere describes and substantiates, and at the same time contrives to make the physical detail an index to character. The reader is led both to see Tulkinghorn and to interpret his appearance. More than that : Tulkinghorn and Vholes, in every aspect of their existence, are a comment on the legal system they represent. The adjectives appropriate to their clothing or appearance are appropriate also to the Law : old-fashioned, secretive, unhealthy, sinister, bloodless, emotionless, stealthy, predatory. The metaphorical force of Dickens's descriptions carries over from characterisation to theme.

The major 'respectable' figure to be defined to a significant extent by his clothes is Mr Dombey. Forster's *Life* shows how concerned Dickens was that Dombey should be suitably presented by the illustrator; and the reason for this concern is easy to understand. The novel obviously posed serious technical problems. When it begins Paul has only just been born, Walter Gay has barely left school, Florence is about six years old, and Mrs Dombey dies. Dickens has to keep the narrative moving by trickery and rhetoric until the children are old enough to take an active part in the story. It's a pretty desperate business : Walter's infatuation for the infant Florence would be distasteful if it were not absurd. The one character who is old enough and forceful enough to take a major role from the beginning is Dombey himself. But Dombey cannot have been easy to dramatise. He has no friends to confide in. He is unemotional, and proudly reserved. His chief occupation is waiting for his son to grow up. Despite the title of the novel Dombey's business life is a complete nullity : a dozen chapters pass before the reader enters his office. It is essential to the author's purpose that his protagonist's personality should be vividly realised, but he has left himself only limited means of projecting it. Appearance counts for a very great deal, and Mr Dombey's appearance is largely a matter of his clothes. When he first addresses Florence, in Chapter I : 'The child glanced keenly at the blue coat and stiff white cravat, which, with a pair of creaking boots and a very loud ticking watch, embodied her idea of a father. . . .' Dickens repeats, but develops, the description in the account of Paul's christening : 'The stiff and stark fire-irons appeared to claim a nearer relationship than any- thing else there to Mr Dombey, with his buttoned coat, his white cravat, his heavy gold watch-chain, and his creaking boots.' The stiffness of the cravat, of course, suggests the stiffness of Mr Dombey's personality; but Dickens is carrying the metaphor far beyond this obvious point. Dombey is made to seem metallic, robot- like. His clothes are rigid, and his clothes are part of himself. The ticking of the watch, the creaking of the boots are mechanical noises. He moves round, in his easy chair, 'as one piece, and not as a man with limbs and joints'; he turns his head in his cravat, 'as if it were a socket'. After the first few chapters specific references to clothes aren't numerous; but by then, as with Tulkinghorn, the adjectives which describe the personality have come to imply the dress : 'formal', 'stately', 'stiff with starch'. And in any case Dombey's haughty stance, his finely tailored, perpendicular garments, and in particular the high cravats that seem to force his head upwards and backwards, have been splendidly caught by 'Phiz'. When, in Chapter XL, Dickens writes at length about 'the cold hard armour of pride' in which Mr Dombey 'lived encased', the metaphorical discussion gains an almost literal force from the visual context Dickens has established.

Having given these examples of what I take to be a controlled and relevant use of information concerning clothes, I must admit that Dickens is often willing, especially in his earlier novels, to insert lengthy descriptions of dress that have no serious function. Some minor character makes a single brief appearance, and Dickens, with imaginative energy to spare, gives him a suit of clothes. Beyond acknowledging the existence of such cases I have nothing to say about them; but I would like to comment on what would seem to be an extended exercise in redundancy of this kind, and that is the characterisation of Sarah Gamp. Mrs Gamp has very little to do with the plot of *Martin Chuzzlewit,* and she has no relevance to such themes as that novel might conceivably be thought to take up. She is, in herself, redundant. Her appeal for Dickens, and for his readers, obviously lay in her eloquence; but for that very reason one might assume that her clothes could scarcely matter – she can speak her mind. We are given all sorts of other information as well. Dickens shows her at her professional duties and in her social role.

He takes us round her apartment and gives us a close look at her furnishings. He tells us quite a lot about her eating and drinking habits. Yet, though he displays her from all these points of view, he still chooses to devote a great deal of space to her clothes and effects – to her snuffy black gown, her shawl, her bonnet, her umbrella and her bundles.

The conventional account of the portrayal makes the essential point : obviously Dickens knows that his story has thrown up a marvellous character and he cannot resist making the most of her, at whatever cost to narrative balance and probabilities. But the case is more complex than such a summary would suggest. Not only are Mrs Gamp's clothes described; they take on a life of their own. Because she sells the funeral weeds she gets from her various employers, 'the very fetch and ghost of Mrs Gamp, bonnet and all, might be seen hanging up, any hour in the day, in at least a dozen of the second-hand clothes shops about Holborn'. On night duty she produces 'a watchman's coat, which she tied round her neck by the sleeves, so that she became two people; and looked, behind, as if she were in the act of being embraced by one of the old patrol'. When she wakens and sits up she projects on the wall 'the shadow of a gigantic night constable, struggling with a prisoner'. Some of her 'rusty gowns' hang from her bed-posts : '. . . and these had so adapted themselves by long usage to her figure, that more than one impatient husband coming in precipitately, at about the time of twilight, had been for an instant stricken dumb by the supposed discovery that Mrs Gamp had hanged herself'. Surprising and entertaining as these passages are, what is most remarkable about them is their appropriateness to the characterisation as a whole. Since she has so small a part to play in the action of the novel, Mrs Gamp might be expected to be a sort of narrative cul-de-sac. But acquaintance with her brings us into contact with numerous other characters : the real-life Betsey Prig, the imaginary Mrs Harris, the deceased Mr Gamp, the Gills, Master Gamp, Mrs Harris's niece. It is as though her work as a midwife had stimulated her to a chronic fecundity. The tendency of her clothes to shape themselves into other people, or into duplicate copies of herself, runs exactly parallel to the activities of her imagination. Mrs Gamp may be extrinsic to the plot of *Martin Chuzzlewit*, but no detail within the characterisation is redundant. Her extraordinary garments reflect her extraordinary mind.

Dickens demonstrated in many of his novels his sense of the powers that clothes can have in themselves. Jingle, Harmon, Headstone, Magwitch, Carton, Darnay, Lady Dedlock, Jonas Chuzzlewit and Tom Gradgrind are some of the many who borrow an outfit for purposes of impersonation or disguise. It is largely a new suit of clothes that transforms Montague Tigg into Tigg Montague. Pip looks for a similar transformation at the hands of Mr Trabb. Some characters are shown to be allergic to certain kinds of dress. Joe Gargery is reduced to panic-stricken inanity by his best clothes. For a long time Pip struggles in vain to disguise Magwitch :

> Whatever he put on, became him less (it dismally seemed to me) than what he had worn before. To my thinking there was something in him that made it hopeless to attempt to disguise him. The more I dressed him, and the better I dressed him, the more he looked like the slouching fugitive on the marshes.

As some of these references will have suggested, *Great Expectations* is a novel in which a strong emphasis is put on clothes. Yet none of the characters is defined by what he wears in the sense that Mr Dombey or Mr Tulkinghorn is so defined. The interest here is thematic. Exaggerated concern with dress is a social phenomenon; and Dickens exposes distortions and stresses in the social system by showing the extraordinary power that clothes have acquired. They can inspire shame or envy. They can change a man's character, or change the way in which he is regarded. As Joe is denatured by his best suit, so Pip has a new personality imposed on him by Mr Trabb. Throughout the novel Dickens finds natural occasion to describe clothes : Biddy's down-at-heel shoes, Miss Havisham's wedding-dress, the mildewed garments that Pip's Newgate guide has bought from the executioner, the bloated boots of the Jack of the causeway, Magwitch's boat-cloak. As with the references to hands and handshakes, the effect is partly structural. One such detail recalls another, to produce an intricate pattern of cross-reference which is part of the meaning of the novel. Dickens has found, in the visual aspect of his work, a means of embodying Forster's plea : 'Only connect.'

V

Mrs Gamp's umbrella is only the most famous of an enormous miscellany of accoutrements and 'portable property' that Dickens distributes among his characters. These possessions often reveal more about their owners than do the clothes they wear. A man whose suit gives nothing away may disclose himself in his watch. In *David Copperfield*, for example, Mr Murdstone's brutality and

Dora's pettishness are objectified in their respective dogs. Miss Murdstone's purse, which shuts up 'like a bite', the 'heavy chain' on which it hangs, and the 'numerous little steel fetters and rivets' with which she adorns herself all serve to identify her as a gaoler. In each of these cases there are elements of psychological and sexual suggestion too complex to be briefly elucidated. But, then, each of the characters concerned is developed at some length, is shown in a variety of situations and is allowed to articulate his or her own feelings. The dog or the purse only fills out the picture. To see the full potentiality of Dickens's method of characterisation through objects, it is more appropriate to consider a personality whose role in the novel is small, and whose articulacy is severely limited.

Barkis makes only half a dozen appearances in *David Copperfield*, before dying about halfway through the narrative. He speaks very little : 'as to conversation, he had no idea of it but whistling'. It is characteristic both of his taciturnity and of his indirection that he should propose to Peggotty, to whom he has 'never said six words', by means of the cryptic message 'Barkis is willin' ' relayed through the infant David. Given his restricted role in the novel and his extremely limited capacities Barkis might remain no more than an entertaining caricature, like the even less communicative Bunsby in *Dombey and Son*. In fact, however, the motives, notions and feelings that can never find their way into Barkis's speech are intriguingly implied by other means, and chiefly by the account of his box. It is first mentioned almost incidentally :

. . . and then I found out that Mr Barkis was something of a miser, or, as Peggotty dutifully expressed it, was 'a little near', and kept a heap of money in a box under his bed, which he pretended was only full of coats and trousers. In this coffer, his riches hid themselves with such a tenacious modesty, that the smallest instalments could only be tempted out by artifice. . . .

Later, when he is bedridden, he repeats to David, who has come to see him, this fiction about the clothes. In honour of the visit he produces a guinea to buy 'something good to eat and drink', but only after taking elaborate measures to preserve his secret. He gets rid of David and Peggotty on the pretext of taking a nap, endures 'unheard-of agonies in crawling out of bed' to get the coin, and finally claims to have discovered it under his pillow. At this stage the box is not a particularly interesting detail : it merely helps to show how 'close' Barkis is in both popular senses of the term. Nor is the metaphor original within *David Copperfield* itself. Miss Murd-

stone has already been described as owning 'two uncompromising
hard black boxes' that are 'never seen open or known to be left
unlocked'. About Barkis's box, however, we are to learn more.
When David next visits Yarmouth, Barkis is dying. He has had the
box 'placed on the chair at the bedside, where he . . . embraced it,
night and day'. After his death it is opened, and proves to contain
more than merely clothes and money :

> I may claim the merit of having originated the suggestion that
> the will should be looked for in the box. After some search, it
> was found in the box, at the bottom of a horse's nose-bag; wherein
> (besides hay) there was discovered an old gold watch, with chain
> and seals, which Mr Barkis had worn on his wedding-day, and
> which had never been seen before or since; a silver tobacco-
> stopper, in the form of a leg; an imitation lemon, full of minute
> cups and saucers, which I have some idea Mr Barkis must have
> purchased to present to me when I was a child, and afterwards
> found himself unable to part with; eighty-seven guineas and a
> half, in guineas and half-guineas; two hundred and ten pounds,
> in perfectly clean Bank notes; certain receipts for Bank of
> England stock; an old horseshoe, a bad shilling, a piece of
> camphor, and an oyster-shell. From the circumstance of
> the latter article having been much polished, and displaying
> prismatic colours on the inside, I conclude that Mr Barkis had
> some general ideas about pearls, which never resolved themselves
> into anything definite.

A first reaction might be that this inventory is agreeably eccentric;
but there is a good deal more to it than that. The nosebag and the
horseshoe, of course, are reminders of Barkis's work as a carrier.
Other objects are more interestingly suggestive. It should be noted,
to start with, that David lists not the contents of the whole box, but
merely of the nosebag. The lemon and the oyster-shell carry the
recession one stage farther, being compartments within the nosebag
within the box. It isn't easy to comment on them without making a
graceful hint sound pretentious and sentimental. Inside the sour
lemon lurks a miniature tea-party, inside the proverbially close
oyster a romantic sheen of pearl. The 'impenetrable secret of the
box' involves Barkis's uncommunicated fancies and the suppressed
generosity that finally leaves his wife and friends well provided.

Money was always one of Barkis's enthusiasms. The other
observable ones were food and Peggotty. It is worth recalling that
his courtship, to which he was first stimulated by the taste of

Peggotty's cakes, was conducted by means of objects rather than words, and represented an obvious combination of these interests. The 'little bundles' that he used regularly to leave behind the door included :

> a double set of pigs' trotters, a huge pin-cushion, half a bushel or so of apples, a pair of jet earrings, some Spanish onions, a box of dominoes, a canary bird and cage, and a leg of pickled pork.

By way of a love-trophy he tore off the bit of wax-candle which Peggotty kept for her thread.

It seems likely that the account of the box evolved in response to a narrative need. Barkis and Peggotty live extremely uneventful lives, yet David must be given *something* to say about them when he makes his Yarmouth visits. Dickens improves on his earlier hints about Barkis's meanness and his box in order to send him off in style. The obvious gain is that a quiet corner of the narrative is pleasantly illuminated, and that there is a point of rest and re-assurance before the shock of Emily's elopement. But the passage also contributes to some of the novel's important general effects. Its picturesque redundancy of detail is characteristic of Dickens's descriptions throughout. Here is the interior of Mr Peggotty's boat, for example :

> It was beautifully clean inside, and as tidy as possible. There was a table, and a Dutch clock, and a chest of drawers, and on the chest of drawers there was a tea-tray with a painting on it of a lady with a parasol, taking a walk with a military-looking child who was trundling a hoop. The tray was kept from tumbling down, by a bible; and the tray, if it had tumbled down, would have smashed a quantity of cups and saucers and a teapot that were grouped around the book. On the walls there were some common coloured pictures, framed and glazed, of scripture subjects; such as I have never seen since in the hands of pedlars, without seeing the whole interior of Peggotty's brother's house again, at one view. Abraham in red going to sacrifice Isaac in blue, and Daniel in yellow cast into a den of green lions, were the most prominent of these. Over the little mantel-shelf, was a picture of the Sarah Jane lugger, built at Sunderland, with a real little wooden stern stuck on to it; a work of art, combining composition with carpentry, which I considered to be one of the most enviable possessions that the world could afford.

Dickens wishes to say not merely that the place is neat and respect-able but that it has personality, that it reflects the tastes, the imagination, the way of life of its inhabitants. The obvious risk he runs in descriptions of this kind is that, if his invention falters, the effect will be of arbitrary 'quaintness' and he will seem sentimental or even patronising. The risk is compounded by the fact that Dickens's dislike of the meanly calculating can lead him to imply that impractical possessions are in themselves signs of grace. Traddles's belief that a flower-pot and stand constitute a useful first step towards furnishing his house is supposed to seem endearing rather than idiotic. In the account of the boat-house, however, and generally throughout *David Copperfield*, Dickens's eye and judg-ment are true. Collectively his descriptions convey a sense of respect for human variety, oddity and unpredictability. The money Barkis leaves in his box shows him to have been provident, but not necessarily anything more. It is the nosebag, the lemon, the oyster-shell and the rest that suggest kindliness, affection and individuality.

Chapter 5

Rooms and Houses

A new chapter in a novel is something like a new scene in a play; and when I draw up the curtain this time, reader, you must fancy you see a room in the George Inn at Millcote, with such large-figured papering on the walls as inn rooms have : such a carpet, such furniture, such ornaments on the mantel-piece, such prints; including a portrait of George the Third, and another of the Prince of Wales, and a representation of the death of Wolfe. All this is visible to you by the light of an oil-lamp hanging from the ceiling, and by that of an excellent fire, near which I sit in my cloak and bonnet; my muff and umbrella lie on the table, and I am warming away the numbness and chill contracted by sixteen hours' exposure to the rawness of an October day : I left Lowton at four o'clock A.M., and the Millcote town clock is now just striking eight.

Charlotte Brontë, Jane Eyre

In an old house, dismal dark and dusty, which seemed to have withered, like himself, and to have grown yellow and shrivelled in hoarding him from the light of day, as he had, in hoarding his money, lived Arthur Gride. Meagre old chairs and tables of spare and bony make, and hard and cold as misers' hearts, were ranged in grim array against the gloomy walls; attenuated presses, grown lank and lantern-jawed in guarding the treasures they inclosed, and tottering, as though from constant fear and dread of thieves, shrunk up in dark corners, whence they cast no shadows on the ground, and seemed to hide and cower from observation. A tall grim clock upon the stairs, with long lean hands and famished face, ticked in cautious whispers; and when it struck the time in thin and piping sounds like an old man's voice, rattled, as if t'were pinched with hunger.

Charles Dickens, Nicholas Nickleby

The room is a large and lofty one, with an ample mullioned oriel window at one end; the walls, you see, are new, and not yet painted; but the furniture, though originally of an expensive sort, is old and scanty, and there is no drapery about the window. The crimson cloth over the large dining-table is very threadbare, though it contrasts pleasantly enough with the dead hue of the plaster on the walls; but on this cloth there is a massive silver waiter with a decanter of water on it, of the same pattern as two larger ones that are propped up on the sideboard with a coat-of-arms conspicuous in their centre. You suspect at once that the inhabitants of this room have inherited more blood than wealth. . . .

George Eliot, Adam Bede

They gradually ascended for half a mile, and then found themselves at the top of a considerable eminence, where the wood ceased, and the eye was instantly caught by Pemberley House, situated on the opposite side of a valley, into which the road with some abruptness wound. It was a large, handsome, stone building, standing well on rising ground, and backed by a ridge of high woody hills; – and in front, a stream of some natural importance was swelled into greater, but without any artificial appearance. Its banks were neither formal, nor falsely adorned. Elizabeth was delighted. She had never seen a place for which nature had done more, or where natural beauty had been so little counteracted by an awkward taste. They were all of them warm in their admiration; and at that moment she felt, that to be mistress of Pemberley might be something!

Jane Austen, Pride and Prejudice

The house in which he lived was of two storeys; a brass plate on the door showed the inscription, 'Hodgson, Dial Painter'. The window on the ground-floor was arched, as in the other dwellings at this end of the street, and within stood an artistic arrangement of wax fruit under a glass shade, supported by a heavy volume of Biblical appearance. The upper storey was graced with a small iron balcony, on which straggled a few flower-pots. However, the exterior of this abode was, by comparison, promising; the curtains and blinds were clean, the step was washed and whitened, the brass plate shone, the panes of glass had at all events acquaintance with a duster. A few yards in the direction away from the Square, and Tysoe Street falls under the dominion of dry-rot.

George Gissing, The Nether World

Both of us were able to look in by standing on the basement, and clinging to the ledge, and we saw – ah! it was beautiful – a splendid place carpeted with crimson, and crimson-covered chairs and tables, and a pure white ceiling bordered by gold, a shower of glass-drops hanging in silver chains from the centre, and shimmering with little soft tapers.

Emily Brontë, *Wuthering Heights*

He hadn't known . . . that he should 'mind' so much how an independent lady might decorate her house. It was the language of the house itself that spoke to him, writing out for him, with surpassing breadth and freedom, the associations and conceptions, the ideals and possibilities of the mistress. Never, he flattered himself, had he seen anything so gregariously ugly – operatively, ominously so cruel. . . . He had never dreamed of anything so fringed and scalloped, so buttoned and corded, drawn everywhere so tight, and curled everywhere so thick. He had never dreamed of so much gilt and glass, so much satin and plush, so much rosewood and marble and malachite. But it was, above all, the solid forms, the wasted finish, the misguided cost, the general attestation of morality and money, a good conscience and a big balance. These things finally represented for him a portentous negation of his own world of thought – of which, for that matter, in the presence of them, he became as for the first time hopelessly aware. They revealed it to him by their merciless difference.

Henry James, *The Wings of the Dove*

There was then a great silence in Castle Rackrent, and I went moping from room to room, hearing the doors clap for want of right locks, and the wind through the broken windows that the glazier never would come to mend, and the rain coming through the roof and best ceilings all over the house, for want of the slater whose bill was not paid; besides our having no slates or shingles for that part of the old building which was shingled, and burnt when the chimney took fire, and had been open to the weather ever since.

Maria Edgeworth, *Castle Rackrent*

By the bye, I have as yet given no description of the old eccentric's abode – an unpardonable omission, I suppose, in these days of Dutch painting and Boz. But the omission was correct, both historically and artistically, for I had as yet only gone to him for books, books, nothing but books; and I had been blind to everything in his shop but that fairyland of shelves, filled in my simple fancy with inexhaustible treasures, wonder-working, omnipotent, as the magic seal of Solomon.

Charles Kingsley, *Alton Locke*

But the complexion even of external things seemed to suffer transmutation as her announcement progressed. The fire in the grate looked impish – demoniacally funny, as if it did not care in the least about her strait. The fender grinned idly, as if it too did not care. The light from the water-bottle was merely engaged in a chromatic problem. All material objects around announced their irresponsibility with terrible iteration. And yet nothing had changed since the moments when he had been kissing her; or rather, nothing in the substance of things. But the essence of things had changed.

                    Thomas Hardy, *Tess of the d'Urbervilles*

Anne saw nothing, thought nothing of the brilliancy of the room. Her happiness was from within.

                    Jane Austen, *Persuasion*

1

Every aspect of description that has been discussed so far has been related, in the first instance at least, to characterisation. With the transition from the individual personality to what lies outside it, the subject grows unwieldy. The potentialities and the problems multiply. In the endlessly miscellaneous area of furnishings, fittings and decoration the question of what, when and how the novelist should describe is an extremely intricate one. At the simplest level a man's living-quarters may, like his clothes, represent an extension of his identity. Many a character in fiction is appropriately and effectively introduced by an account of his living-room. Mr Dombey's mansion changes internally and externally in accordance with his fluctuating fortunes and aspirations. Mrs Clennam's home, gloomy and crippled like herself, collapses when her life collapses. Each of these houses is seen as a projection of the owner's personality; but the kind of suggestion involved goes deeper than that discussed in the preceding chapter. Clothes display style or taste; the permanence of bricks and mortar allows for something more. Pemberley, Mansfield Park, Hamley Hall, Castle Rackrent, Lowick Manor, Wuthering Heights – each, in its way, stands for a way of life, for values.

But there is a limit to the amount of space that the novelist can usefully allot to definition of this kind. Too much static description will clog his narrative. The values which Merton Densher sees expressed in Maud Lowder's rooms are to be crucially significant to the developing plot. James makes his descriptive point briskly enough, and proceeds to his story. But many a novelist is a good deal more haphazard and prolix with such commentaries. In the second chapter of *Mary Barton* Mrs Gaskell devotes more than five hundred words to an exhaustive account of the Bartons' living-room. She describes the layout – front door, rear doors, window, stairs and fireplace – the furniture, the curtains, the crockery, the decorations. Her paragraph concludes : '. . . if you can picture all this with a washy, but clean stencilled pattern on the walls, you can form some idea of John Barton's home'. The author would seem to have divided intentions here. Since she is writing about a mode of living she knows to be quite unfamiliar to most of her readers, she provides additional descriptive help to enable them to participate imaginatively in the story. But the chapter in question contributes nothing to the action of that story; it is a self-contained piece of reporting, a sociological sketch. Mrs Gaskell wants to show us a typical, rather than a particular, weaver's house and hospitality. But the episode might still have had some direct expository useful-ness if the information it contained were later to be recalled, to be *used*. How often in the novel is Mary seen to draw the 'blue-and-white check curtains', or fetch coal from 'the slanting closet under the stairs'? Although the chapter adds a little, in general terms, to our knowledge of the Bartons, it is mainly of interest now as a fragment of social history.

Mrs Gaskell's fault here is a venial one, both in kind and in scale. There are far worse offenders. It is so much easier for the novelist to begin a description of décor than to know when to stop. In *The Old Wives' Tale*, for instance, Arnold Bennett includes a great deal of redundant detail of this kind. His book could be handsomely abridged without essential loss. At least when he is describing 'the actual draper's shop of the Baines's' that he had lived in as a child his interiors have some sociological or period relevance; but even here the relevance is too slight and the material too copious. It is more apparent that the author himself is familiarly at home in the shop than that his characters are. Some of the passages concerned might have contributed usefully to an autobiography or memoir by Bennett, but they have no real function in his novel. This is aimless realism.

In all the cases mentioned so far in the chapter the starting-point has been character. The author says, in effect : 'Such are the surroundings that this person has created for himself.' But most of the action in most novels takes place on neutral territory. The room in which characters meet and talk may mean nothing to either of them, may not be perceived by them : it is no more than a stage for their encounter. The novelist can supply simply such visual detail as will help the reader to set the scene in his imagination. And these details need not be numerous. Usually it is not the room as a whole, but a small section of it, that constitutes the arena. A sufficient answer to the question 'Where does this dialogue take place?' may be: 'On the stairs'; 'At the breakfast-table'; 'By the window'. Where this amount of contextual information is provided, the characters have objects to relate to, defined movements to make. The advice about descriptive writing that Chekhov gives through Trepliov in *The Seagull* might be adapted to this rather different problem. Here the purpose is to suggest, not a romantic outdoor scene, but an ordinary interior. The focusing detail needs less to be evocative than to be solid, practical, *usable*. Beside the fire Carker (and later Steerforth) can start 'beating the coals softly with the poker'. At a toilette-table Rosamond Vincy will study her reflection in the glass. Kneeling by the sofa Anne Elliot is vulnerable to the assault of little Walter Hayter. And in helping to establish a situation these properties become more substantial in their own right. If the fireplace or the sofa is adequately 'there', the reader will take the rest of the room on trust.

This very fact, however, involves an imaginative difficulty of a curious kind, which I do not remember seeing discussed. In their dialogue and authorial comment the great Victorian novels are closer to us, more immediate in their language and manner, than any other literature produced before this century. Many of the observations of Mr Bennet, Harold Skimpole, Michael Henchard, Gwendolen Harleth or, for that matter, of Jane Austen or George Eliot could still be made, word for word, today. We need make no adjustment, it might seem, for convention or lapse of time. The familiar tones tend to make us forget that the voices are speaking in the past – in that foreign country where things are done differently. We are in danger of being beguiled into an anachronistic response. One obvious safeguard is that the reactions of the ear might be modified by those of the eye. But how often is the student of nineteenth-century fiction induced to visualise an almost completely alien world? How often is he made to recall that the city streets he is reading about are thronged with horse-drawn vehicles? that the drawing-rooms are over-furnished and over-decorated in the heavy Victorian manner? Again these are elusive questions. Who can be categorical about what he sees from the corner of his mind's eye? But my feeling is that many famous novels of the period have, with the passage of time, become open to misconstruction through descriptive insufficiency. Sights that would have been commonplace to the author and his contemporary readers were taken for granted. Everyone knew what a busy street or a middle-class drawing-room looked like. Why should the novelist waste words in describing them? But these commonplace sights have radically changed. Drawing-rooms are transformed to sitting-rooms. Coal-fires give way to central heating. Mantelpieces have been cleared, carpets taken up, pictures taken down. Our furnishings differ from those of our great-grandparents in quantity, shape and weight. In the absence of adequate descriptive promptings it is all too easy for us to forget the extent of these changes. The instinctive response is to set the familiar voices of nineteenth-century fiction in fairly familiar surroundings. The room we visualise, or half-visualise, may be remote from anything that the author could have conceived. We hear with him, but we do not see with him – and in consequence we may subtly misjudge what his characters are doing and saying.

Perhaps so abstruse an idea might be better introduced in positive rather than in negative terms. *Wives and Daughters* is a novel that conveys a particularly clear sense of domestic appearances and activities. It is one of the few works of Victorian fiction that show how people lived from day to day, how they passed a summer afternoon or an autumn evening. The very fullness here exposes, by contrast, a certain scantiness in the work of some of Mrs Gaskell's contemporaries. Elsewhere domestic staff are frequently anonymous – even invisible. In *Wives and Daughters* the servants have names and personalities : they are part of the household. Again and again Mrs Gaskell's evening scenes are carefully lighted – by candles, or by a fire, or by both. As a result they are shadowed, softened, 'placed', where an equivalent scene from a novel visually vaguer may seem, to the imagination of the modern reader, to be sharply illuminated, as by electric light. The descriptive detail that sustains our feeling for context must surely refine our response to meaning and tone. Its absence must, to an extent, disable us.

Descriptive deficiency is naturally more apparent when the setting in question is such that we cannot unthinkingly reconstruct it in twentieth-century terms. A case in point is the Netherfield ball in *Pride and Prejudice*. Some chapters previously, in response to Miss Bingley's suggestion that it would be more rational to base such functions on conversation, Darcy has made the famous reply: 'Much more rational, my dear Caroline, I dare say, but it would not be near so much like a ball.' Yet in the event, oddly (or ironically?) enough, the Netherfield ball is almost exclusively a conversation piece. There is no description of the room, or of the dancing, or of the ladies' dresses. We never learn how, or by whom, the music is provided. Elizabeth's dances with Darcy in effect involve no physical movement at all, but consist merely of dialogue. In contrast the charity ball in *Wives and Daughters* is described in some detail. The music comes from a band comprising 'two violins, a harp, and an occasional clarionet'. The rooms are decorated with evergreens and artificial flowers. Most of the women wear dark silks, but Molly is in white muslin, Cynthia in pink, and Lady Cumnor in black velvet. There is a similar specificity in George Eliot's much briefer account of the private dance at Park House in *The Mill on the Floss*. The party occupies a whole suite – a library, a long drawing-room, a sitting-room and a conservatory. Waltzes alternate with country dances, 'under the inspiration of the grand piano'. Maggie is dressed in black, Lucy in white. Despite differences of aim and focus both Eliot and Gaskell provide sufficient visual information to enable and encourage the modern reader to set about imagining a nineteenth-century ball. The scene from *Pride and Prejudice* offers practically nothing to the eye.

But the comparison cannot be left there. For all its visual limitations Jane Austen's chapter is by far the most brilliant of the three. Although it flows so freely, it has been put together with extreme intricacy. The ball is a crucial episode in the novel, a turning-point for all the main characters. There is scarcely an incident recorded by the author, scarcely one fragment of talk, that is not relevant to future developments and charged with irony. It is only at a second reading that one can begin to appreciate just how rich and complex the scene is. Yet even at a first reading, and at the simplest narrative level, we are unlikely to feel that the chapter is descriptively inadequate. The several stages of the evening are duly marked : arrival, talk, dancing, supper, singing, more dancing, departure. There are many encounters, exchanges, tensions, developments. The episode works superbly in terms of equivalence. By the time the Bennets leave Netherfield the reader has had, so to speak, an ample ball's-worth of varied experience.

The argument is still not closed, however, for the chapter might contain all that it does contain and yet have also the visual dimension that Eliot and Gaskell provide. Set aside the difficulties of the modern reader. Even from the point of view of her contemporaries Jane Austen's chapter might have seemed curious in its failure to mention any of the features of the ball that the participants might have been particularly expected to enjoy. There is no sense that the music or the dancing could be exhilarating. Molly Gibson taps her foot when the little band strikes up; Maggie Tulliver is deeply stirred by the dancing and the flowers and the lights. But the omission of such suggestions from the *Pride and Prejudice* chapter is not an accidental consequence of a faulty descriptive method. For Elizabeth Bennet, as for her creator, the sensual aspects of life must be considered relatively unimportant. Jane Austen duly emphasises those things that her heroine would most care about. Neither background description nor the absence of it can ever be devoid of significance, because a novelist's characters are tacitly defined by what they do or do not perceive.

II

Overcombe Mill, in *The Trumpet-Major*, is an outstanding example of 'solidity of specification'. Repeatedly and variously described, it becomes a powerful presence in the novel. The emphasis proves to be amply justified, because the mill is far more than a mere background, or environment, for the story. Hardy makes it directly relevant to his plot, his theme, and even to his tone.

Few authors are so skilful at starting a novel. In both *Tess* and *The Mayor of Casterbridge* the action begins with the opening page. Hardy has virtually eliminated the need for exposition, by devising an initial situation that is both self-explanatory and inherently dynamic. In *The Trumpet-Major* it is the mill, in effect, that provides such a situation. When the soldiers arrive in Overcombe 'The Mill Becomes an Important Centre of Operations', because the Dragoons water their horses twice daily at the pond. And since the Garlands share the Lovedays' house it is inevitable that Anne should be thrown into regular contact, first with John, and later with Bob. The courtship that constitutes most of the action of the novel can be carried forward, easily and naturally, by chance encounters in the garden, or small social events. Proximity fosters affection between Mrs Garland and the Miller; and with their marriage the separate living-quarters are united into a still more appropriate arena for amorous pursuit, hide-and-seek with the press-gang, and manoeuvres with Uncle Benjy's box.

The mill can be frequently described, then, because it is frequently *used*. If the story were set in another house it would have to be a different story. Although Hardy's control of his plot is sometimes lax, particularly towards the close, his descriptive references to the mill are persuasive in their circumstantial consistency. The black beams that Matilda Johnson admires in Chapter XVII are first alluded to in Chapter V. The brooks and the apple-trees in the garden are mentioned repeatedly, and it is into an apple-tree that Bob leaps to escape the press-gang. The chimneys, the ladders, the corner-cupboard, the clock, the lattice windows are all featured more than once. Even the slugs in the garden, the subject of lively discussion in Chapter XIX, have made a preliminary appearance nine chapters previously. The ordinary reader, of course, doesn't check up on these recurrences; but they offer him tacit reassurance that Hardy has thoroughly imagined his fictitious mill, and knows his way round it.

The mill lends itself to repeated description because Hardy has made it worth describing. It is not only a picturesque, but also a palpable environment. A fine mist of flour hangs in the air, and settles on windows and furnishings. The scent of Miller Loveday's pipe comes down Mrs Garland's chimney. In some 'worm-eaten cupboards' linger 'layers of ancient smells'. Hardy is always marvellously adept at describing sound; and the mill is a rich source of sounds. There is the 'music' of the wooden cogs – 'the big wheel began to patter and the little ones to mumble in response'. Outside there is the noise of the mill-race and of the brooks in the garden. When it rains : 'The surface of the mill-pond leapt up in a thousand spirts under the . . . downfall, and clucked like a hen in the rat-holes along the banks as it undulated under the wind.' The reader becomes so acclimatised to the sounds that, in the aftermath of Bob's escape from the press-gang, Hardy is able to make a positive point about the silence that uncannily prevails because the mill has been stopped.

There is another, and more unusual, sense in which the mill is made actively present in the story. Hardy gives it literally a life of its own : he makes it the centre of an ecological system. There are ants, slugs and snails in the garden, rats and eels in the river. When Mrs Garland spring-cleans the house for Bob's wedding she sweeps away moths, wood-lice, death-watch beetles and flour-worms. Among the familiar sights that Bob surveys on his return from sea are 'the meal lodged in the corners of the window-sills, forming a soil in which lichens grew without ever getting any bigger, as they had done since his dimmest infancy; the mosses on the plinth towards the river, reaching as high as the capillary power of the walls would fetch up the moisture . . .'. It comes naturally to Hardy to see human life as but an aspect of a larger life, and to treat every manifestation of that larger life with respect. When Anne goes to her casement with a candle : 'The light shone out upon the broad and deep mill-head, illuminating to a distinct individuality every moth and gnat that entered the quivering chain of radiance stretching across the water. . . .' Hardy can think quite unironically of the 'distinct individuality' of a gnat. Elsewhere in his fiction he implies

an affinity between man and minnow, man and insect – even
between man and fossil. He sympathises with the Garlands and the
Lovedays, but he never quite forgets that they are only five out of
the innumerable inhabitants of the mill and its environs. There is a
teeming life all around them.

As I suggested in the previous chapter, *The Trumpet-Major*, even
by Hardy's own standards, is unusually concerned with historical
perspective. Overcombe Mill helps him to make his point. It is an
ancient building. The threshold has been 'worn into a gutter by the
ebb and flow of feet that had been going on there ever since
Tudor times'. There are reminders of the past everywhere, some of
which Mrs Garland cleans away :

By the widow's direction the old familiar incrustation of shining
dirt, imprinted along the back of the settle by the heads of countless jolly sitters, was scrubbed and scraped away; the brown circle
round the nail whereon the miller hung his hat, stained by the
brim in wet weather, was whitened over; the tawny smudges of
bygone shoulders in the passage were removed without regard to
a certain genial and historical value which they had acquired.

These human traces go the way of the moths and the flour-worms.
Hardy establishes an atmosphere of transience, gentle, and even
soothing, that harmonises with the very workings of the mill : 'The
water, with its flowing leaves and spots of froth, was stealing away,
like Time, under the dark arch. . . .' The operations of Time on the
characters, as on the mill itself, are not too terrible. Mrs Garland is
wrinkled round the eyes, and has had 'some worn-out nether mill-
stones' abstracted by the dentist; but she can still win the hand of
Miller Loveday. Matilda Johnson is past her first bloom, but she
contrives a lucky marriage with Festus. Anne and both her suitors
must be dead by the time the story is told; but the mill still stands.
Hardy speaks of visiting it himself. *The Trumpet-Major* is an
attractive novel largely because it is so delicately placed and stylised.
The characters are defined in terms of costume, but the house they
live in is substantial, and alive, and enduring. Hardy involves us in
his story; but his descriptions of the mill, like his descriptions of
costume, skilfully limit and control that involvement.

III

Solomon Gills's shop, crammed with telescopes, charts, maps,
sextants, quadrants and so forth, is so truly nautical in its character

that it seems 'almost to become a snug, sea-going, ship-shape concern, wanting only good sea-room, in the event of an unexpected
launch, to work its way securely to any desert island in the world'.
Dickens returns to this fantasy in his last novel, where Mr Tartar's
chambers have similarly 'a sea-going air' : '. . . the whole concern
might have bowled away gallantly with all on board, if Mr
Tartar had only clapped to his lips the speaking trumpet that was
slung in a corner, and given hoarse orders to heave the anchor up,
look alive there, men, and get all sail upon her!' But between
Dombey and *Edwin Drood* Dickens carries the idea a stage farther,
by making Mr Peggotty and his adopted family actually live in a
beached converted boat, so situated that the young David can fancy
'that the sea might rise in the night and float the boat away . . .'.

This device is so brilliantly apt to its context that the reader tends
to take it for granted. Of course the Peggottys live in a boat. Where
else would they live? It takes a positive effort of critical imagination
to uninvent the boat. The obvious residence for the family would
have been some cottage on the sea-front; and no doubt Dickens
could have devised one appropriately whitewashed, fishy and sea-
weedy. But it is hard to believe that any mere cottage could have
been made to contribute so much to the novel. Peggotty's boat,
though we see it only seldom, is one of the great homes of English
fiction.

Dickens has some difficult technical problems to solve in the
third chapter of *David Copperfield*. Yarmouth is to play a vital part
in the story; somehow it must be given identity, atmosphere. David's
future will be closely bound up with the future of the Peggottys;
somehow the Peggotty family, and Mr Peggotty in particular, must
be made to appear attractive and interesting. This cannot have
been a simple task. Mr Peggotty is *good*, of course – 'as good as
gold and as true as steel' – but he has little to say during David's
visit, and almost nothing to do. The boat solves both problems
simultaneously. Yarmouth acquires far more character than either
Dover or Canterbury, because its sea-faring, ship-building, fish-
catching aspects are all expressed in Peggotty's isolated dwelling.
Betsey Trotwood's house has really nothing to do with Dover, but
Peggotty's house *is* Yarmouth. Its interior decorations have a con-
centratedly nautical flavour. Not only is there a painting of a lugger
over the mantelshelf – the ship starts out of the canvas, because it
has 'a real little wooden stern stuck on to it'. The mirror in David's
room is framed with oyster-shells, and his table bears 'a nosegay of
seaweed'. Above all, the air is so permeated by the scent of the
shellfish in which Peggotty deals that 'when I took out my pocket-

handkerchief to wipe my nose, I found it smelt exactly as if it had wrapped up a lobster'. The effect of all these details is powerfully synaesthetic : the boat is an Oxo-cube of marine associations. Everything that Dickens might have wanted to tell us about Yarmouth is contained within it.

Part of the description of the interior was quoted in the preceding chapter, in the discussion of Barkis's box. The boat is Peggotty's box, and he lives inside it. The pictures and fittings are part of his personality. Peggotty is mixed up with all the sights and sounds and smells that David encounters during his short stay. The simple cheerful man gains colour and authority from his connections with the sea :

> As slumber gradually stole upon me, I heard the wind howling out at sea and coming on across the flat so fiercely, that I had a lazy apprehension of the great deep rising in the night. But I bethought myself that I was in a boat, after all; and that a man like Mr Peggotty was not a bad person to have on board if anything did happen.

The metaphor here is already almost an actuality. Peggotty's boat is 'a sort of ark'; and he has given refuge to the orphaned Ham and Emily, victims of the sea. Later the 'great deep' is indeed to rise and sweep the family away. When Steerforth has figuratively destroyed their home Dickens shows it literally shattered by the storm. But Daniel Peggotty survives, and again rescues Emily. The two of them are able to sail away with Mrs Gummidge in another boat, to a new life.

The reader doesn't need any great critical penetration to follow the workings of this metaphor. In the second half of the novel it is probably made over-explicit. My brief comment on it is merely a means towards making another point about David's first trip to Yarmouth. The chapter seems so spontaneous, so easy and fresh, so undesigning, that one can imagine a critic of an earlier generation using it as an example of Dickens's careless prolix inventiveness. Orwell might have quoted the description of the interior of Peggotty's boat as evidence of the author's delight in 'unnecessary detail'. Yet now the episode plainly seems intrinsic to an elaborate metaphorical design. The immediacy of Dickens's descriptive writing, so far from being at odds with his growing interest in pattern and structure, is vital to it. His mature novels develop the metaphors that he had always, instinctively, seen in the visible world about him.

But the boat poses an interesting problem. Although it seems to be minutely described, vividly realised, it defies the imagination. As depicted by 'Phiz' the inverted vessel could barely accommodate a midget. In the plate entitled 'Little Emily' the 'delightful door cut in the side' appears to be only slightly higher than a nearby barrel. Emily herself would be able to stand upright only directly below the keel. When 'Mrs Gummidge casts a damp on our departure' the boat looks rather larger, but is still grossly inadequate to Peggotty's needs. The doorway, which would present difficulties of proportion and verticality, has been tactfully eliminated. In his illustrations of the interior 'Phiz' makes room for the inhabitants and their visitors by a trick of perspective, widening out the foreground immensely. The interior he devises is quite irreconcilable with the exterior.

My guess is that few readers of *David Copperfield* will be able to make what should theoretically be the obvious reply to these objections – which is that the illustrations are false to the text. A close look at the chapter suggests that Dickens clearly intended the boat to be the right way up. In my experience most students, at any rate, fail to notice this discrepancy; and the failure does not surprise me. It is natural to apprehend, and to apprehend vividly, all the copious detail that Dickens provides, and yet still be unable to say whether the boat is upside-down. Somehow the description is simultaneously very specific and very insubstantial.

A number of other notable houses in Dickens have the same characteristic. Wemmick's home, in *Great Expectations*, is literally a castle, with drawbridge, turret, gothic windows, and flagstaff. Nearby he has 'a separate fortress, constructed of lattice-work', which encloses the gun he fires every night. He also grows cucumbers, keeps pigs, fowls and rabbits, and enjoys smoking a pipe in his bower, beside an ornamental lake. There are excellent thematic reasons for the defensive, domestic and romantic aspects of Wemmick's residence; but, although the various details are severally conceivable, the reader can't plausibly assimilate them into one property. The proportions are wrong; the different elements don't mix. When closely imagined, Wemmick's castle collapses.

Satis House, in the same novel, presents a rather different case. The courtyard, the brewery and the garden are solid terrain. There is scope for Pip to wander, explore and fight. But the house is another matter. To try to picture its interior with any precision – the shrouded windows, the pitch-dark passages and stairs, the rotting bride-cake – would be as futile as to attempt to imagine the day-to-day life of its owner. The real world ends at Miss Havisham's front door.

In the case of each of these dwellings – Peggotty's, Wemmick's, and Miss Havisham's – the physical details that are supplied add up, not to a credible home of wood or brick, but to an outer shell of personality, an enclosing idea. Dickens makes us see these residences rightly, distracts us from a literal view, by stylistic sleights not unlike the tricks of perspective that 'Phiz' uses when depicting the interior of Peggotty's boat. Dickens sheds some light on the purpose and the workings of his device in *Little Dorrit*, where he has one of his characters practise it on her own account. Mrs Plornish has embellished her parlour wall with 'a little fiction' :

This poetic heightening of the parlour consisted in the wall being painted to represent the exterior of a thatched cottage; the artist having introduced (in as effective a manner as he found compatible with their highly disproportionate dimensions) the real door and window. . . . No Poetry and no Art ever charmed the imagination more than the union of the two in this counterfeit cottage charmed Mrs Plornish. It was to her nothing that Plornish had a habit of leaning against it as he smoked his pipe after work, when his hat blotted out the pigeon-house and all the pigeons, when his back swallowed up the dwelling, when his hands in his pockets uprooted the blooming garden and laid waste the adjacent country. To Mrs Plornish, it was still a most beautiful cottage, a most wonderful deception; and it made no difference that Mr Plornish's eye was some inches above the level of the gable bedroom in the thatch.

Mrs Plornish loves the cottage because it stands for the idyllic life that she and her husband would like to lead, and perhaps, in a sense, do lead. It cannot be accommodated, in literal terms, to the actualities of their existence : as with Peggotty's boat, the proportioning is full of contradictions. But the artist has done his best to hide the discrepancies; and in any case Mrs Plornish knows how the cottage should be viewed. She doesn't believe in its reality, but she does believe in its truth. The circumstantial detail – flowers, chimney-smoke, 'a cloud of pigeons', a dog – are means of expressing that truth, rather than attempts to deceive the eye. Though if they could deceive the eye as well, of course, so much the better.

Dickens describes many a house or room, I think, in something like this spirit. The technique is closely related to his methods of describing clothes and possessions. But as the object depicted becomes larger and more external, so the distortion from normality is liable to be exposed. An eccentric watch or walking-stick strains nobody's credulity. An eccentric dwelling-place, though much more obviously expressive, can strike the reader as implausible – not a single oddity, but a museum of oddities. But Wemmick's castle and Peggotty's boat suggest the possibility of a saving grace. If the map you consult shows adequately the European countries you happen to be concerned with, you will care very little that it greatly magnifies Greenland. So with the novel : where a central character is sufficiently convincing, the reader can fairly easily adjust to the fact that his home, narrowly considered, appears rather larger, or rather smaller, than life.

IV

I believe the argument advanced in this section to be essentially true; but I will express it hyperbolically – partly for the sake of definition, partly as a challenge to the reader to make out a counter-case.

In Chapter 2 of *Middlemarch* Dorothea Brooke meets Mr Casaubon for the first time, the occasion being a dinner-party at Tipton Grange. The episode is a compact one, and sets the narrative moving briskly. Dorothea, of course, is immediately drawn to Casaubon, although the other guest, Sir James Chettam, tries hard to win her attention. There is little authorial comment : the characters disclose their personalities by their own words. The speech-styles of Mr Brooke and Mr Casaubon are particularly well defined and revealing. All the energies of the scene, however, are in the dialogue. It could hardly be less of a dinner-party. In fact there are only two phrases within the chapter to establish that the main part of the conversation indeed takes place at the dinner-table:

'Sir Humphry Davy?' said Mr Brooke, over the soup. . . .
In the beginning of dinner, the party being small and the room still. . . .

There is nothing about the house, nothing about the furnishings, nothing about the domestic staff. There is no account of the meal itself, or any attempt to mimic its length or progression. Had the chapter been entitled 'Dinner at the Grange' Eliot might reasonably have gone one step farther, and eschewed descriptive suggestion altogether.

Does the absence of background detail weaken the imaginative impact of the scene? Do we see it, apprehend it, less vividly than the author would have liked? What kind of opportunities does she forgo by concentrating so exclusively on dialogue? Obviously such questions can't be given a categorical answer; but they can at least prompt useful discussion and comparison. To illustrate the alternative narrative method, here is a brief extract from Tolstoy's account, in *Anna Karenin*, of Oblonsky's dinner with Levin at the England restaurant :

> Oblonsky crumpled his starchy table-napkin and tucked a corner of it inside his waistcoat. Then with his arms comfortably on the table he attacked the oysters.
> 'Not bad,' he said, tearing the quivering oysters from their pearly shells with a silver fork and swallowing them one after another. 'Not bad,' he repeated, turning his dewy, brilliant eyes from Levin to the Tartar.
> Levin ate his oysters, though he would have liked white bread and cheese better. But he looked at Oblonsky with admiration. Even the Tartar, after uncorking the bottle and pouring the sparkling champagne into the delicate, wide-lipped glasses, watched Oblonsky with a smile of evident pleasure, while he adjusted his white cravat.
> 'You don't care much for oysters?' asked Oblonsky, draining his wineglass. 'Or are you worried about something? Eh?'
> He wanted Levin to be in good spirits. But it was not that Levin was not in good spirits: he felt constrained. The feelings that filled his heart made him ill at ease and uncomfortable in this restaurant with its private rooms where men were dining with ladies, and all this running to and fro and bustle. The bronzes, the mirrors, the gas-light, and the Tartar waiters were all an affront. He was afraid of defiling the love which filled his soul.[18]

Later the two men are drawn into animated conversation; but at this stage their chief concern – and Tolstoy's – is the meal itself. The food and wine are sensuously described because both Levin and Oblonsky, in their very different ways, are sensuously aware of them. The physical facts of the scene constitute a situation. Levin's mood involves his response to the dinner, to the restaurant, to the waiter, to his friend's enjoyment. Oblonsky delights in the meal, and the whole context of the meal, but notices Levin's constraint. Their discussion grows out of their mutual awareness.

Tolstoy's scene, then, would appear to have been far more fully and richly imagined than its counterpart in *Middlemarch*. The reader is enabled to see as well as to hear. And the descriptive passages, far from being merely an agreeable addition, are integral to the development of the episode. What is thought and said are significantly influenced by what is seen.

It would be foolish to attach too much weight to a single comparison of this kind. Either passage might be unrepresentative. The novelist cannot be consistently circumstantial in his narration, and probably should not try to be. It might be argued on Eliot's behalf that her chapter deals with a sufficiently ordinary social occasion, which most of her readers would be quite capable of imagining for themselves. The meal that Levin and Oblonsky share is specifically an expensive and even exotic one. Again, while each of these men has reason to react strongly to his surroundings, Dorothea Brooke, the character with whom Eliot is principally concerned, is far more responsive to intellectual than to sensual stimulus. Celia might notice the food and the drink and the silverware, as she notices Casaubon's white moles; Dorothea's interest is in the conversation.

But when these points have been conceded it is still possible to feel that Eliot's chapter is descriptively too scanty. It has no visual dimension at all. The conversation might equally well be taking place at a tea-party, or during a walk. Our sense of intellectual or emotional inter-play is surely diminished by the lack of physical inter-play. Several sources of information are denied us. We learn something about Oblonsky from seeing what he eats, and how he eats. Casaubon only talks.

There is more at issue here than the vitality of a single scene. To explain its physical nullity in terms of Dorothea's asceticism is perhaps to imply a weakness in the novel as a whole. Her temperament and values are such that her appearances have a numbing effect on the narrative : she tends to create a circumstantial vacuum. In one sense this is a point that Eliot specifically wishes to make. When Dorothea first visits Lowick there is a fairly detailed description of 'the bow-windowed room' that Celia urges her sister to take :

To bow-window looked down the avenue of limes; the furniture was all of a faded blue, and there were miniatures of ladies and gentlemen with powdered hair hanging in a group. A piece of tapestry over a door also showed a blue-green world with a pale stag in it. The chairs and tables were thin-legged and easy to upset. It was a room where one might fancy the ghost of a tight-laced lady revisiting the scene of her embroidery. A light book-case contained duodecimo volumes of polite literature in calf, completing the furniture.

This room, unlike the dining-room at Tipton Grange, is effectively realised. It reveals a good deal about the life that Dorothea may expect after her marriage. But she scarcely sees what is before her eyes. When Mr Brooke hints that she might introduce 'some new hangings, sofas, and that sort of thing', his niece 'eagerly' rejects the idea : 'Pray do not speak of altering anything. . . . I like to take these things as they are.' This is the habit of mind that makes her interesting – but it also makes her less amenable to Eliot's character-istic method of fictional portrayal. Since her physical surroundings say very little to her or about her they are often left undescribed. Maggie Tulliver and Gwendolen Harleth move amid settings, furnishings, objects that help to define them. Few novelists have been so sensitive and adept in exploring this kind of inter-relation-ship. By contrast Dorothea, whose driving impulses are more exclusively mental and spiritual, is condemned to dwell in an environment of authorial comment. If George Eliot seems over-indulgent to her heroine, as Professor Leavis has suggested, the reason may be methodological rather than psychological.

This does not mean that the realist writer must necessarily find it difficult to portray self-denial. The trouble with Dorothea's brand of asceticism is that it seems facile, and therefore uninteresting. Her 'inner life' is insulated from so many of the problems, temptations and stimuli that the 'outer life' presents for most of us. Again, Tolstoy's approach is very different here. The scene in the England restaurant provides a clear illustration of his habitual method in *Anna Karenin.* Each of the participants has something on his mind: Oblonsky is worried about the rift with Dolly; Levin is preoccupied with thoughts of Kitty. These anxieties colour, but certainly do not dull, their reactions to what they see and hear. Each man is responding simultaneously to his private thoughts, to the immediate setting, and to his friend. A similar complexity is built into episode after episode in the novel. There is never a single focus of interest. Each moral or emotional problem has to be redefined to take account of the miscellaneous circumstances that seem to accumulate round it. The visual and sensual energy of the restaurant scene implies not only the vitality of the men involved, but also the diversity and untidiness of the experiences that make up their lives. Oblonsky's case is the less interesting, in that his primary object is always pleasure. For him the meeting with Levin means first and foremost a good meal. Levin, however, is Dorothea's equivalent – a man whose dominant ever-present concern is his desire to live rightly, to 'live for his soul'. Even this one account of a dinner suggests that his struggles will be harder and more instructive than

Dorothea's, because it shows how far he is from being naturally ascetic. Levin does not happen to care for expensive restaurants or champagne and oysters, but he likes and admires Oblonsky, who delights in such things. Here is another contradiction to add to the many his mind has been grappling with. Oblonsky's tastes may differ from his own, but they must at least be imaginable for him, since he keenly relishes a variety of physical enjoyments. Skating, shooting, or even mowing give him an intense feeling of well-being. The truth he seeks must take account of such experience. He could not found a morally healthy life on mere abstinence and negation.

By contrast Dorothea's range of experience and responsiveness seems narrow. Two important areas of her life have been left virtually blank. It is probably anachronistic to speculate as to whether she had, or ever hoped to have, a happy sexual relationship with her husband. But the question of Casaubon's possible impotence is a vital one, because in deciding to marry him Dorothea must surely have taken conscious account of the likelihood or unlikelihood of bearing him children. Is her childlessness a sacrifice, a disappointment, or a relief? In the ambiguous circumstances her pallid reaction to Celia's baby might seem to imply some general lack of physical warmth. But a still odder omission is the absence of any adequate account of Dorothea's devotional life. We see little in the way of prayer or meditation, or even of good works – though she talks a good deal about cottages. Her spiritual intensity has to be taken on trust, since Eliot finds so little for her to *do*.

It matters all the more, therefore, that Dorothea enjoys so few incidental activities or interests that might convey a suggestion of mental or physical energy. Her self-denial seems less admirable than it was apparently meant to, because the self that is denied is so undemanding, so colourless. The more worldly, more trivial Gwendolen Harleth sings well, rides well, and is an accomplished archer. She has acting talent enough to think of the stage as a possible career. She flirts and gambles. In conversation she is quick, witty, sometimes audacious. If she is ever to live the better life she craves, these potentialities, these tastes, skills and appetites must somehow be subdued or reconciled. This is what makes her spiritual struggle absorbing to us.

Part of the problem with Dorothea is that her self-abnegation sets in too soon. She is one of many characters in Victorian fiction whose past is effectively a blank. If her years in Lausanne are given slightly more retrospective substance than Clym Yeobright's stay in Paris or Arthur Clennam's in China, that is all that can be said for them. What reader of *Middlemarch* remembers Madame Poinçon? When the novel begins, Dorothea's girlhood is over. George Eliot offers a page or two of exposition, and then leaves her heroine's former life and character to inference. The first dramatised scene is excellent because the conflict it contains is appropriately suggestive. Dorothea is genuinely divided between distrust of ornament and her sense of the beauty of her mother's emeralds : 'All the while her thought was trying to justify her delight in the colours by merging them in her mystic religious joy.' Her self-deception and her flash of temper help to bring her to life. But beyond this point renunciation is too rapid, easy and far-reaching. She abandons riding before we have seen her on a horse. Her speedy marriage deprives her of nearly all the obvious pleasures of young womanhood; but George Eliot avoids direct indications of frustration or sense of loss. In effect Dorothea has relinquished the enjoyments of a Gwendolen Harleth or a Maggie Tulliver for the sake of marital and spiritual aspirations that George Eliot is reluctant to scrutinise or to pursue. The inner life remains insubstantial; the outer life, in terms of physical activity or sensual awareness, almost ceases to exist.

Levin's search for self-fulfilment will not allow him to ignore experience of any kind. His omnivorousness justifies and even demands the density of narrative texture that characterises Tolstoy's novel. In narrowing Dorothea's ideals Eliot narrows the descriptive range of the major story in *Middlemarch*. Where Dorothea goes the story thins – there is nothing to see or to touch.

V

Although Mansfield Park means so much to Fanny Price, the house takes on little reality for the reader as a building. We never once see it from the outside. The drawing-room, in which much of the action takes place, is not described. Most of the novel is made up of conversations and arguments, but few of these are set in a physical context. Our general impression of the place must derive from the observations of Mary Crawford, who sees 'a spacious modern-built house, so well placed and well screened as to deserve to be in any collection of engravings of gentlemen's seats in the kingdom, and wanting only to be completely new furnished . . .'. Only the East room, Fanny's private domain, is given some décor, some atmosphere; and the few details concerned do so much to illuminate her quiet existence that one is inclined to regret the descriptive frugality elsewhere. But it is easy to see what Jane Austen is about. For her, as for Fanny, Mansfield Park is more an idea, a way of life, than a handsome house in a large estate.

By contrast Fanny's Portsmouth home is described in some physical detail, because it is the physical facts of her family's day-to-day existence that she finds demoralising :

> There was neither health nor gaiety in sun-shine in a town. She sat in a blaze of oppressive heat, in a cloud of moving dust; and her eyes could only wander from the walls marked by her father's head, to the table cut and knotched by her brothers, where stood the tea-board never thoroughly cleaned, the cups and saucers wiped in streaks, the milk a mixture of motes floating in thin blue, and the bread and butter growing every minute more greasy than even Rebecca's hands had first produced it. Her father read his newspaper, and her mother lamented over the ragged carpet as usual, while the tea was in preparation. . . .

The passage has been justly praised for its realism, its perceptiveness, and its economy. In a few lines it sums up most of the miseries that Fanny has had to endure : slovenliness, dirt, discomfort, seedy food, the inefficiency of the maid, the unruliness of the children, the inattentiveness of her parents. The only major trial it omits is the deafening noise made by all the inmates of the house, and exaggerated by the smallness of the rooms and the thinness of the walls. Fanny cannot help comparing her parents' house with Mansfield Park, and finding that the comparison is wholly in favour of the latter.

Some readers, and especially those whose childhood environment was of the Portsmouth rather than of the Mansfield Park variety, may feel that there is something snobbish in Fanny's preference. This meek girl, constantly concerned to do what is right, rejects her own impoverished family in favour of wealthy relatives. But one must beware of a superficial judgment here. Fanny has been separated from her parents for years, and finds, when she is reunited with them, that they care very little for her. They reject her before she rejects them. Being constitutionally delicate she is physically distressed by bustle and noise. The standards and manners she has acquired over the previous eight years are irrelevant and unappreciated in her parents' home. Altogether it is only honest and reasonable in her to conclude that she would be happier and more comfortable in Mansfield Park.

The problem is that she concludes a good deal more than that. The comparisons she draws between Portsmouth and Mansfield are unfair and morally confused. Here are two of the relevant passages :

No, in her uncle's house there would have been a consideration of times and seasons, a regulation of subject, a propriety, an attention towards every body which there was not here.

. . . she could think of nothing but Mansfield, its beloved inmates, its happy ways. Every thing where she now was was in full contrast to it. The elegance, propriety, regularity, harmony – and perhaps, above all, the peace and tranquillity of Mansfield, were brought to her remembrance every hour of the day, by the prevalence of every thing opposite to them *here*.

The reader can hardly help remembering that Mansfield was totally unlike Fanny's recollection of it. Its 'beloved inmates' repeatedly reduced her to tears by their thoughtlessness, selfishness and even cruelty. As Henry Crawford asks his sister : 'Was there one of the family, excepting Edmund, who had not in some way or other continually exercised her patience and forbearance?' So far from there being 'attention towards every body', Fanny was usually ignored. Nor was she alone in having cause for discontent. Sir Thomas is so unpopular a father that no one is sorry to see him depart for Antigua. His return reduces Mansfield social life to 'sameness and gloom . . . a sombre family-party rarely enlivened'. Fanny recalls to Edmund that this glumness had always prevailed in the past : 'There was never much laughing in his presence . . . I cannot recollect that our evenings formerly were ever merry, except when my uncle was in town.' Mrs Norris is spiteful. Tom is a wastrel, who prefers to stay away from his father. Maria and Julia are frequently at loggerheads, and eventually Maria is driven into a disastrous marriage partly by 'hatred of home'.

It is understandable that Fanny's recollections of her uncle's house should be coloured by nostalgia – that she should think kindly even of the less agreeable Bertrams. What is repellent is the double standard. Towards the Prices she is ruthlessly censorious :

She could not respect her parents, as she had hoped. On her father, her confidence had not been sanguine, but he was more negligent of his family, his habits were worse, and his manners coarser, than she had been prepared for. . . . She might scruple to make use of the words, but she must and did feel that her mother was a partial, ill-judging parent, a dawdle, a slattern, who neither taught nor restrained her children, whose house was the scene of mismanagement and discomfort from beginning to end, and who had no talent, no conversation, no affection towards herself. . . .

Most of these criticisms of Mrs Price are equally applicable to Lady Bertram – it is a point that Jane Austen herself makes, in effect, in a later chapter. But when does Fanny assess her cousins, her uncle, or either of her aunts with anything like this degree of frankness? She would presumably plead their kindness; but such kindnesses as they have offered have cost them so little in terms of expense or effort that her thankfulness seems quite disproportionate. When Sir Thomas so much as asks a servant to light a fire for her in the East room she is excited to 'even painful gratitude'. Her feelings towards the Bertram family aren't easily to be distinguished from the sycophancy of the poor relation. It is as though she gives them moral credit for having money. In this context her response to her cramped Portsmouth bedroom is revealing : 'She soon learnt to think with respect of her own little attic at Mansfield Park, in *that* house reckoned too small for anybody's comfort.' She comes to feel not merely gratitude but 'respect' for an attic that none of the Bertrams would dream of using. If this hint of a confusion of values seems accidental, it is amply confirmed in the succeeding chapter, when Fanny is recalling Mansfield :

> If tenderness could be ever supposed wanting, good sense and good breeding supplied its place; and as to the little irritations, sometimes introduced by aunt Norris, they were short, they were trifling, they were as a drop of water to the ocean, compared with the ceaseless tumult of her present abode.

What Fanny thinks of here as 'little irritations' the reader knows to have been acts of meanness, envy, and calculating malice. Fanny is comparing wickedness with noise – and warmly preferring the wickedness because it causes her less discomfort. The unpleasant aspects of her life at Portsmouth are material, or are material in their origin. Yet she is far more critical about them than about the various kinds of moral nastiness that she has encountered among her cousins. Nearly everything she dislikes about her parents' way of living could be put right with money. The family could move to a larger house with thicker walls, and hire efficient servants to keep it clean. Fanny could have a room to herself, and her father a study in which to read his newspaper. The children could be kept out of sight and out of hearing, and could 'cut and knotch' the furniture in their own quarters. Even in the East room at Mansfield the furnishings 'had suffered all the ill-usage of children' – the little Prices are not exceptional in their destructiveness. It is perfectly comprehensible that Fanny should feel unhappy and out of place at

Portsmouth, but it is shocking that her reaction should be so obtusely egocentric. She proves unable or unwilling to see the causal connection between poverty and impropriety.

The issue is a sensitive and intriguing one, because it lies close to the centre of Jane Austen's moral teaching. She has been widely praised for the wisdom and tact which enable her to reconcile a scrupulous concern with conduct and a realistic appreciation of the importance of an adequate income. She brings social and moral instruction into alignment by showing that good manners, properly understood, are the social application of morality. But there are moments in most of her novels where the equation comes to seem a little glib. The Portsmouth section of *Mansfield Park* confirms the suspicion that the virtues Jane Austen most frequently praises – order, propriety, decorum – are virtues that money can buy and poverty may be unable to afford. The Bertrams can afford them, and so win Fanny's uncritical devotion. The Prices cannot, and are therefore despised.

It would appear, then, that the main effect on Fanny of her visit to Portsmouth is precisely that envisaged by Sir Thomas. His idea was 'that a little abstinence from the elegancies and luxuries of Mansfield Park, would bring her mind into a sober state. . . . Her Father's house would, in all probability, teach her the value of a good income. . . .' One has only to reread the passage to be certain that Jane Austen cannot have intended merely to corroborate so crass a view. But, then, what has gone wrong? Where this author seems confusing or confused it is usually advisable to seek out ironic reservations that may have been overlooked. Is there any suggestion that Fanny's response to Portsmouth is mistaken or inadequate? Jane Austen may be fond of her heroine, but she has made it plain that Fanny is by no means morally infallible. There *is*, in fact, an implied rebuke to Fanny in the conduct of her energetic sister, Susan : 'Susan tried to be useful, where *she* could only have gone away and cried. . . .' Somehow this girl has survived her upbringing. Her resolute character is Fanny's 'first solid consolation . . . for the evils of home'.

But when this point has been taken there would still seem to be no doubt that Fanny Price is generally in the right. The novel only makes sense on the basis that Mansfield Park stands for some important values concerning family life, values which we see upheld by Sir Thomas, still more by Edmund, but most of all by the meek Fanny Price. Jane Austen intended, surely, not that the asperities of Portsmouth life should accomplish Sir Thomas's crude aims, but that they should enable Fanny to feel more passionately her commitment to the values that Mansfield has taught her. She must inevitably hate Portsmouth, because it is so remote from the Mansfield ideal – an ideal that is to be vindicated through her own conduct, even if some of the Bertrams fail to live up to it.

That last clause, of course, is by way of being an understatement. By the end of the novel the married Maria has run away with Henry Crawford, Julia has eloped with the wretched Yates, and Tom's character has been redeemed only at the eleventh hour by a near-fatal illness. The limitations of the Bertram parents and of Aunt Norris have been severely exposed. Even Edmund has been shown to be dangerously fallible. The 'idea' of Mansfield Park may have survived, but it has taken a bad battering.

By contrast, and against all the odds, the Price family emerge triumphant, despite the noise, the indiscipline and the bad diet. The bold Susan actually aspires to take Fanny's place as minister to 'the hourly comfort of her aunt'.

In *her* usefulness, in Fanny's excellence, in William's continued good conduct, and rising fame, and in the general well-doing and success of the other members of the family, all assisting to advance each other, and doing credit to his countenance and aid, Sir Thomas saw repeated, and for ever repeated reason to rejoice in what he had done for them all, and acknowledge the advantages of early hardship and discipline, and the consciousness of being born to struggle and endure.

'The advantages of early hardship.' Strange point and new! What has hardship to do with the 'elegance, propriety, regularity, harmony' of Mansfield Park? At the last minute Jane Austen has thrown in her hand. The way of life and method of upbringing that her novel seemed designed to endorse have produced a good deal of vice and misery; the environment whose ugliness and bad influence she has been at pains to expose she allows to have fostered moral character and healthy development. *Mansfield Park* surely ends in inconsistency, if not in downright confusion; but I cannot believe that many readers find that a cause for complaint. A consistent conclusion that did nothing to redress the chilly priggishness of Fanny's dishonest reflections on her parents' home would surely have been much more damaging to our sense of Jane Austen's fairness and generosity of mind.

Chapter 6

Villages and Towns

The little town of Great Winglebury is exactly forty-two miles
and three-quarters from Hyde Park corner. It has a long,
straggling, quiet High-street, with a great black and white clock
at a small red Town-hall, half-way up – a market-place – a cage
– an assembly-room – a church – a bridge – a chapel – a theatre
– a library – an inn – a pump – and a Post-office.

Charles Dickens, *Sketches by Boz*

The Green lay at the extremity of the village, and from it the
road branched off in two directions, one leading farther up the
hill by the church, and the other winding gently down towards
the valley. On the side of the Green that led towards the church,
the broken line of thatched cottages was continued nearly to the
churchyard gate; but on the opposite, north-western side, there
was nothing to obstruct the view of gently-swelling meadow, and
wooded valley, and dark masses of distant hill.

George Eliot, *Adam Bede*

The towering rock, the houses above houses, one man's doorstep
rising behind his neighbour's chimney, the gardens hung up by
one edge to the sky, the vegetables growing on apparently almost
vertical planes, the unity of the whole island as a solid and single
block of limestone four miles long, were no longer familiar and
commonplace ideas. All now stood dazzlingly unique and white
against the tinted sea, and the sun flashed on infinitely stratified
walls of oolite. . . .

Thomas Hardy, *The Well-Beloved*

It was a pretty large town, with an open square which they were
crawling slowly across, and in the middle of which was the Town-
hall, with a clock-tower and a weather-cock. There were houses
of stone, houses of red brick, houses of yellow brick, houses of lath
and plaster; and houses of wood, many of them very old, with
withered faces carved upon the beams, and staring down into

the street. These had very little winking windows, and low-arched doors, and, in some of the narrower ways, quite overhung the pavement. The streets were very clean, very sunny, very empty, and very dull. A few idle men lounged about the two inns, and the empty market-place, and the tradesmen's doors, and some old people were dozing in chairs outside an alms-house wall; but scarcely any passengers who seemed bent on going anywhere, or to have any object in view, went by; and if perchance some straggler did, his footsteps echoed on the hot bright pavement for minutes afterwards. Nothing seemed to be going on but the clocks, and they had such drowsy faces, such heavy lazy hands, and such cracked voices that they surely must have been too slow. The very dogs were all asleep, and the flies, drunk with moist sugar in the grocer's shop, forgot their wings and briskness, and baked to death in dusty corners of the window.

Charles Dickens, *The Old Curiosity Shop*

Treby Magna . . . had been, at the beginning of the century, quite a typical old market-town, lying in pleasant sleepiness among green pastures, with a rush-fringed river meandering through them. Its principal street had various handsome and tall-windowed brick houses with walled gardens behind them; and at the end, where it widened into the market-place, there was the cheerful rough-stuccoed front of that excellent inn, the Marquis of Granby, where the farmers put up their gigs, not only on fair and market days, but on exceptional Sundays when they came to church. And the church was one of those fine old English structures worth travelling to see. . . .

Such was the old-fashioned, grazing, brewing, wool-packing, cheese-loading life of Treby Magna, until there befell new conditions, complicating its relation with the rest of the world, and gradually awakening in it that higher consciousness which is known to bring higher pains. First came the canal; next, the working of the coal-mines at Sproxton, two miles off the town; and, thirdly, the discovery of a saline spring, which suggested to a too constructive brain the possibility of turning Treby Magna into a fashionable water-place.

George Eliot, *Felix Holt*

It was a town of red brick, or of brick that would have been red if the smoke and ashes had allowed it; but as matters stood it was a town of unnatural red and black like the painted face of a savage. It was a town of machinery and tall chimneys, out of which interminable serpents of smoke trailed themselves for ever and ever, and never got uncoiled. It had a black canal in it, and a river that ran purple with ill-smelling dye, and vast piles of building full of windows where there was a rattling and a trembling all day long, and where the piston of the steam-engine worked monotonously up and down like the head of an elephant in a state of melancholy madness. It contained several large streets all very like one another, and many small streets still more like one another, inhabited by people equally like one another, who all went in and out at the same hours, with the same sound upon the same pavements, to do the same work, and to whom every day was the same as yesterday and tomorrow, and every year the counterpart of the last and the next.

Charles Dickens, *Hard Times*

For several miles before they reached Milton, they saw a deep lead-coloured cloud hanging over the horizon in the direction in which it lay. It was all the darker from contrast with the pale gray-blue of the wintry sky; for in Heston there had been the earliest sign of frost. Nearer to the town, the air had a faint taste and smell of smoke; perhaps, after all, more a loss of the fragrance of grass and herbage than any positive taste or smell. Quick they were whirled over long, straight, hopeless streets of regularly-built houses, all small and of brick. Here and there a great oblong many-windowed factory stood up, like a hen among her chickens, puffing out black 'unparliamentary' smoke, and sufficiently accounting for the cloud which Margaret had taken to foretell rain. As they drove through the larger and wider streets, from the station to the hotel, they had to stop constantly; great loaded lurries blocked up the not over-wide thoroughfares. Margaret had now and then been into the city in her drives with her aunt. But there the lumbering vehicles seemed various in their purposes and intent; here every van, every wagon and truck, bore cotton, either in the raw shape in bags, or the woven shape in bales of calico. People thronged the footpaths, most of them well-dressed as regarded the material, but with a slovenly looseness which struck Margaret as different from the shabby, threadbare smartness of a similar class in London.

Elizabeth Gaskell, *North and South*

A very long walk was before her. She wished to get as far as the Strand bookshops, not only for the sake of choice, but because this region pleased her and gave her a sense of holiday. Past Battersea Park, over Chelsea Bridge, then the weary stretch to Victoria Station, and the upward labour to Charing Cross. Five miles, at least, measured by the pavement.

George Gissing, *The Odd Women*

Well, we were in the provinces, and no error. I mustn't name the place, because there's this fool convention in English publishing that you don't name the place you're writing about, in case the unpleasant characters in the story turn out to resemble the mayor's in-laws or whatever. Neither, on the other hand, am I going to follow the idiotic custom of calling it Bruddersfield or Grim-chester. If I can't name this town, I'll just call it 'the town I mustn't name'. Anyway, it's that place you stop at on the way to Manchester – the one where you look out of the train window when it's slowing down, and think, 'Well, at least I don't live *here*.'

John Wain, The Contenders

I

At Trumpyngtoun, nat fer fro Cantebrigge,
Ther gooth a brook, and over that a brigge,
Upon the whiche brook ther stent a melle;
And this is verray sooth that I yow telle. . . .

The student who consults the appropriate note will discover that *The Reeve's Tale* is set near Cambridge because it is very specifically a rejoinder to *The Miller's Tale*, which was set in Oxford. He will also learn that Trumpington was an actual place, complete with brook, bridge and mill. But the reader who lacks this information may still feel that the story has got off to a good start. Already he has been encouraged to imagine, to visualise. And since 'Cante-brigge', at least, is a real town the Reeve has begun to justify his fourth line : the tale could well be a true one. Circumstantiality of place is a venerable and valuable device of the story-teller. Dickens's Inspector Bucket knows its usefulness : 'I was rather in a hurry . . . for I was going to visit a aunt of mine that lives at Chelsea – next door but two to the old original Bun House. . . .' It is a device dear to the con-man because the opportunity for verification that it seems to offer is in practice delusive. The Canterbury Pilgrims are a long way from Cambridge, and Mercury is unlikely to institute inquiries in Chelsea.

The Reeve's story is a pretty tall one – hence the need for authenticating detail. Yet the novelist who is striving to be 'authentic' throughout his narrative may well find himself embarrassed about the matter of location.

Among other public buildings in a certain town which for many reasons it will be prudent to refrain from mentioning, and to which I will assign no fictitious name, there is one anciently common to most towns, great or small : to wit, a workhouse. . . .

It is because Dickens wants to speak the truth about workhouses that he must prevaricate about the name of the town. Even to imply a particular place might leave him open to legal action by indignant workhouse authorities and an outraged beadle, eager to prove that no child called Oliver Twist has ever been in their care.

The dilemma involved is an interesting one that continues to plague writers of fiction. It concerns not only legal liabilities but also the very nature of the novelist's craft, and the location of the shadowy border-line between story-telling and fact. This book has tried to show how the imaginative writer will tend towards that border-line. With a little simplification his course could be summarised as follows : he invents a character to whom he gives, or tries to give, a believable personality and mode of speech, a believable face, posture and habit of movement. He dresses him in clothes of a certain style and installs him in a certain kind of house. But where is that house to be situated – in St Paul's Crescent, Camden Town, London, or the High Street, Anytown, Loamshire? It is with this decision that the novelist commits himself, or can seem to commit himself, to make-believe or to actuality. What is the point of making your hero convincingly 'real' in so many respects if he is condemned to dwell in a manifestly imaginary world? But, conversely, will not an attempt to involve him with the living world either transform the novel into fake biography, or expose, through juxtaposition, the limitations of the fictional portrayal?

Because of this difficulty, or contradiction, or paradox, my argument can reach no satisfactory conclusion. Just as there are techniques for portraying, and making significant, faces, gestures, clothes, houses, so there are means of 'realising' a town or a village. But technique can only go so far. Ultimately the unreality of the town or village will have to be conceded. Inspector Bucket and the Reeve both address a captive audience; the reader of a novel that juxtaposes fiction and reality will have leisure to test the former against the latter.

The great nineteenth-century novelists, like many other writers before and since, probed this border-line, and attempted forays across it, both for serious purposes and for sport. Bob Loveday has an interview with Captain Hardy, and serves under him at Trafalgar. Colonel Dobbin and his party meet Thackeray, the man who invented them, in Pumpernickel. Many of these jokes or sleights involve place :

As to the town in which Felix Holt now resides, I will keep that a secret, lest he should be troubled by any visitor having the insufferable motive of curiosity.

Dickens and Gissing commonly make their characters live in specific London streets. Tulkinghorn borrows John Forster's home in Lincoln's Inn Fields; Lucetta Le Sueur takes Colliton House in Dorchester. But when Alice, in her travels behind the looking-glass, enters the mirror-image of a shop that still survives in St Aldate's, Oxford, she is served by a bespectacled sheep. What circumscribes all such devices is the hard truth that, however the two are mixed, fact is always vulnerable to fiction, and every reader knows it to be so.

There is another reason altogether why this chapter must differ from its predecessors. The argument of the book moves outwards from the more personal to the less, from the particular to the general. A man's face is part of his identity. He can control his gestures, at least in theory, and select his clothes. If he cannot choose the house he lives in, he may still contrive to impose a style on it. All these factors can reasonably be expected to display his personality, at any rate to some extent. But a man's native town or village, of course, can never reveal his character in this sense; rather it is his character that comments on the town. The assumption I have often made in this book for working purposes – that a novelist starts from character – is obviously simplistic. For many an author the first impulse will be a desire to exhibit a certain place, or a certain way of life. His various characters are means to an end. He says, in effect : 'Here is a group of Londoners : through them you may know London.'

The less there is in the way of social background, the more autonomous the characters will appear to be. An apt example of a truly minimal social environment is provided by *Wuthering Heights.* The name Gimmerton is frequently mentioned, but it never becomes more than a name. The reader can never establish quite where Gimmerton is situated in relation to Thrushcross Grange or Wuthering Heights. He can gain no notion of its size, appearance or population. No character in the novel actually *reaches* Gimmerton; and it is easy to see why. Cathy, Heathcliff and the rest devote themselves single-mindedly to powerful passions. If they went to Gimmerton, shopping or visiting, they would come up against ordinary people, and necessarily appear warped, monstrous, or childish. It is tactful of Emily Brontë to keep them away. A difficulty arises, however, concerning Cathy's decision to marry

Edgar Linton. He has in him so few of the qualities she is shown elsewhere to admire that the attraction would seem inevitably to lie in his social life. Cathy remarks that she looks forward to being 'the greatest woman of the neighbourhood'. But there *is* no neighbourhood. Edgar seems to have no friends, nor any relations save for his unfortunate sister. The Lintons pay no visits and receive no callers. All Edgar has to offer is his library. If the Lintons or the Earnshaws could ever get to Gimmerton their lives would be different and Cathy's marriage choice might seem a real one. On the other hand even a moderate injection of social reality might well prove too much for so intense, so operatic a story. Many of the things Emily Brontë does well she might be prevented from doing at all. Her characters must be isolated in order to be themselves.

George Eliot's preoccupation with environment, with 'the medium in which a character moves', places her work at the opposite extreme to Emily Brontë's. Her characters are explained, are created, by the milieu in which they live, or the milieu in which they have been brought up. But already that alternative suggests the complexity of her deterministic views. Asked to write an essay on the importance of environment in Eliot's novels nine students out of ten would turn, quite reasonably, to *Middlemarch*. Their emphasis would be on her skill in creating a sense of a community of people with certain habits, beliefs, prejudices, superstitions; in making the reader see how the aspirations of a Dorothea or a Lydgate can be stifled by public opinion, by the gossip of Mr Chichely, Dr Sprague, Mrs Cadwallader, the Mawmseys, Toller, Wrench, Bambridge and the rest. But there is a further, and very different, aspect to the question. Eliot remarks in *Daniel Deronda* :

A human life, I think, should be well rooted in some spot of a native land, where it may get the love of tender kinship for the face of earth . . . a spot where the definiteness of early memories may be inwrought with affection, and kindly acquaintance with all neighbours, even to the dogs and donkeys, may spread not by sentimental effort and reflection, but as a sweet habit of the blood.

This Wordsworthian belief is strong in Eliot, and is of crucial importance to *The Mill on the Floss*. Though this novel has its own community, a community of aunts and uncles, Maggie's childhood environment is very much a physical one, involving the mill, the river, Yap the terrier, and other animals, toys, insects, cakes and fruit and cowslip wine. The author celebrates, for all of us, the joys of 'that familiar hearth, where the pattern of the rug and the grate and the fire-irons were "first ideas" that it was no more possible to criticise than the solidity and extension of matter'. These are powerful influences, and Eliot makes them appear so, but they work in very indirect and abstract ways. There is a connection between Maggie's eventual fate and the dolls and jam-puffs and floury spiders of her childhood, but it isn't a connection that's easy to demonstrate. In *Middlemarch* and *Daniel Deronda* Eliot ensures that no such problem can arise. Dorothea and Gwendolen are introduced to the reader when newly settled in a fresh environment; their girlhood is left unimagined.

In *Daniel Deronda* Eliot points to yet a third kind of determining influence. When Gwendolen Harleth arrives back at her local railway station from Leubronn she feels that 'the dirty paint in the waiting-room, the dusty decanter of flat water, and the texts in large letters calling on her to repent and be converted, were part of the dreary prospect opened by her family troubles . . .'. Eliot develops the scene at some little length before commenting :

> Contemptible details these, to make part of a history; yet the turn of most lives is hardly to be accounted for without them. They are continually entering with cumulative force into a mood until it gets the mass and momentum of a theory or a motive. Even philosophy is not quite free from such determining influences. . . .

She is not quite consistent here, having told us only a page or two previously how Mirah, in squalid circumstances, 'had grown up in her simplicity and truthfulness like a little flower-seed that absorbs the chance confusion of its surroundings into its own definite mould of beauty'. Mirah is presumably an exception : it isn't given to most of us to grow up like flower-seeds. But the general issue is plain enough. Eliot shows how a shabby environment can have a demeaning effect. Her account of Gwendolen's response to the station points forward to the novels of Gissing.

Eliot proposes, then, at least three distinct ways in which environment can help to determine character. Curiously, none of them involves much sense of a town or village as an architectural or topographical milieu : there is plenty to hear in Middlemarch, but very little to see. Where aesthetic responses are concerned, whether agreeable or disagreeable, the subject is likely to be the countryside rather than anything in a town or village street. The three kinds of environmental pressure are very far from being mutually incompatible. If Eliot usually makes little attempt to reconcile or to relate them it is because of the technical difficulty of the enterprise. She can only do so much at a time.

Her dilemma here must have been familiar to many of her contemporaries. For the eighteenth-century novelist environment was scarcely an issue. It was virtually a prerequisite of a work of fiction that the hero or heroine should be isolated from any normal social context : Tom Jones and Roderick Random are set on the road; Pamela and Clarissa are locked away. In general these characters *see* very little. Even Robinson Crusoe's island remains quite unvisualisable. But for the nineteenth-century novelists it was essential that their characters should relate to an environment of some kind. Indeed, this was the very subject of their work. Their protagonists were no longer shut away in country houses. In Charlotte Brontë's fiction even the heroine had to find herself a job. Dickens, Eliot and Gaskell were all concerned to stress the interrelatedness of different social classes. Their novels had to have large cast-lists, had to convey a sense of community.

But in the nineteenth century, too, Nature was invented. Response to scenery and weather could disclose character. More than that : exposure to certain kinds of scenery could actually modify character. The 'oppressive horizontality' of Egdon Heath affects the personalities of those who inhabit it. Arthur Clennam finds London spiritually destructive :

Nothing to see but streets, streets, streets. Nothing to breathe but streets, streets, streets. Nothing to change the brooding mind, or raise it up.

Wherever his story took him the novelist found no escape from context – and all of it was meaningful. There was simply too much 'stuff' for him to cope with. I was trying to show in earlier chapters that it can be difficult enough to keep the reader reminded of a crooked nose and a pair of green eyes. To sustain an impression of certain streets in a town, of certain houses in those streets and of the relationships and social status of the people who live in the houses, is a massive task indeed. It is not surprising that Eliot should have chosen to show the young womanhood of Dorothea but not the girlhood, and the girlhood of Maggie Tulliver but not the young womanhood. An attempt to describe both kinds of environmental pressure, and to inter-relate them, must have made the texture of the novel far too dense for the story.

A novelist can so depict the face, clothes and manner of a character that the reader fleshes out the simplified portrait with his imagination and notices no artificiality or limitation. But a town, or even a village, presents a problem of a different order. There is simply too much of it : streets, houses, shops, perhaps offices and factories, people, relationships, work, history, gossip, transport. What author could keep all these factors in mind, and find the technical means of implying them in his narrative? All he can hope to do is to fabricate a pattern of suggestions adequate to the more obvious requirements of his novel, and to distract the attention of his readers from the gaps that he must inevitably leave.

II

A road-map of your own country looks comfortably familiar. You have visited many of the towns, driven along many of the motorways. Altogether the map corresponds so consistently with the known reality, in terms of names, boundaries, contours, relative distances, that it can easily be seen as something more than a diagram. There is a lurking feeling that if you were suitably miniaturised by a mad scientist you would find it to be a living replica of the real thing, and as such decently hospitable. An Englishman set down on the microdot containing the town of Dover could strike out confidently, along a main road, for the little polygon marked London.

The equivalent map in a historical atlas is disturbing because it subverts this instinctive sense of familiarity. You see and yet you don't see the country you know. A map of Roman Britain shows the contours and coast-lines of today, but roads, towns and railways are swept away, and the few names that remain are changed. Deposited in this terrain your diminutive double would feel lost and lonely, but his case need not be completely hopeless. From Dubris he could walk along a recognisable line of cliffs. He might even be able to find the Roman road to Londinium. Disagreeably lost in time he could still rely on certain established dimensions and relationships.

Now conceive of a third kind of map. The outline is again that of Britain. Certain present-day names are there – London, Manchester, Birmingham – but alongside them are others of a quite different status : Cranford, Budmouth, Middlemarch, Barchester. For this is a composite map of nineteenth-century English fiction. In this your double would be lost completely, notwithstanding his knowledge of some of the towns, villages and even buildings that occupy the miniature landscape. For travel is impossible – the roads are blocked by invisible barriers. London and Dorchester are separated by distance; London and Durnovaria by distance and time – a vehicle with some sort of Wellsian over-drive might conceivably make the journey. But Casterbridge is inaccessible from London. Car'line Aspent, in Hardy's 'The Fiddler of the Reels', can take a train to London; but we cannot make the return journey with her to Casterbridge.

The fictional map could be very easily compiled. The south-western area would be based on Hardy's Wessex, but would have to incorporate a number of additional towns and villages. Near Exeter would be Barton, from *Sense and Sensibility*; in the New Forest Helstone, from *North and South*. Sanditon would appear on the Sussex coast; Barchester, presumably, between Winchester and Salisbury. A number of real towns would qualify for the map through their incorporation into fiction : Lyme and Bath from *Persuasion*, Dover and Canterbury from *David Copperfield*, London from a score of novels. North of London the map thins a good deal. Dickens provides some outposts in East Anglia : Ipswich and Bury St Edmunds (*The Pickwick Papers*), and Yarmouth (*David Copperfield* again). George Eliot puts a number of towns and villages in the Midlands. Knutsford is represented by Cranford, Manchester by Milton, Preston by Coketown. The most northerly entry would probably be the village of Limmeridge, near Carlisle, from *The Woman in White*.

What, it might be asked, would be the purpose of such a map? From the literary-critical point of view it could serve no purpose whatsoever. But it would represent only an extension of a practice which some of the best novelists of the Victorian period seem to take seriously. Hardy maps not only Wessex but also the Isle of Slingers (for *The Well-Beloved*) and Egdon Heath (for *The Return of the Native*). Eliot makes a skeleton map of the Middlemarch area for her own use. Trollope takes delight in inventing an entire county :

Of *Framley Parsonage* I need only further say, that as I wrote it I became more closely acquainted than ever with the new shire which I had added to the English counties. I had it all in my mind, – its roads and railroads, its towns and parishes, its members of Parliament, and the different hunts which rode over it. I knew all the great lords and their castles, the squires and their parks, the rectors and their churches. This was the fourth novel of which I had placed the scene in Barsetshire, and as I wrote it I made a map of the dear county. Throughout these stories there has been no name given to a fictitious site which does not represent to me a spot of which I know all the accessories, as though I had lived and wandered there.[19]

Many another novelist, less topographically specific than these, will yet be at pains to relate his fictional town or village to real ones in terms of distance – to say that it is seventy-five miles from London, or sixty from Liverpool. It is a curious enterprise, as the whimsicalities at the start of this section were intended to emphasise. The point of a map is to show the relationships between places that exist. In special circumstances – the historical atlas – one can wish to see the relationships between places that used to exist. But there is something vertiginous in the notion of a map that relates real towns and imaginary ones; and the oddity is increased when the 'real town' in question itself becomes, with the passage of time, merely one that used to exist. Yet not only these novelists, but also generations of their readers, have found the attempt to chart such relationships intriguing. It seems to be partly through such simple means that many of the towns and villages of nineteenth-century fiction do take on an eighth or a quarter of a dimension of reality, do come to constitute a hallucinatory landscape that the reader almost feels he can enter.

The endeavour concerned seems, disconcertingly, to be traceable to either of two radically different tendencies. One is the tendency towards make-believe, the desire to carry pretence as far as it can go. Trollope plays with Barsetshire as a child might play with a clockwork railway or a toy farm. The fuller, the more coherent the detail, the more satisfactory the pretence. A model car is more fun if the wheels have rubber tyres and the doors open and shut. The authenticity of the detail doesn't make it any the less a toy. In the same way a fictional town can give pleasure through circumstantial completeness – through having shops, a market-square, a town hall, a Norman church, a railway station with regular services to London. But many a novelist will use similar technical resources in an attempt to fabricate not a toy but a seeming reality. The author who wishes to suggest that to all intents and purposes his characters are living people will want to situate them in what is to all intents and purposes an actual town. Verisimilitude is arguably trivial as an end, but it can be of vital significance as a means.

The fictional places I've been talking about take on different kinds and different degrees of life. Some remain mere names. Dingley Dell is one such example – surprisingly so, since Muggleton is described in a long set-piece. Some come alive as communities of people, although the reader has little sense of the appearance of the streets or buildings. Middlemarch and Cranford are towns of this kind. Quite a number of villages and small towns are sketched at length in an introductory passage but assume no topographical reality. What reader could hope to find his way round Treby Magna, Milton or Cloisterham? By contrast Gissing's London (the point will be developed later) is almost all distances and relationships : the streets are related, but they remain unseen. Casterbridge is a rare example of a town defined visually, topographically, socially and historically.

But all these modes of representation, even the most minimal, might be seen as in some sense realistic. A town or a village can mean quite different things to two different inhabitants, and may be viewed quite differently by them. Some people spend most of their waking hours outdoors while others move between home and office. A taxi-driver knows the streets of a town, a postman the houses, a gasman the insides of the houses. But perhaps no two taxi-drivers, or no two postmen, view their environment in quite the same way. Our perception of the streets we walk down probably varies as much as our perception of eye-colours. To describe the town one lives in is to describe oneself. To invent a town, similarly, is to imply certain beliefs, tastes, sympathies. The environment within which the characters of a novel move will always be something more than mere background.

III

Emma Woodhouse has never seen the sea. She is the only Jane Austen heroine never to escape from her native village. Highbury, the village in question, seems to be very precisely located in Surrey, near Kingston, sixteen miles from London, nine from Richmond, seven from Box Hill. Its layout and character are established in some detail. Highbury is a 'large and populous village almost amounting to a town'. At right-angles 'from the broad, though irregular, main street' runs Vicarage-lane, about a quarter of mile down which lives Mr Elton. Other named thoroughfares include Broadway-lane, the Richmond road, and Donwell-lane, which leads to Donwell Abbey, home of Mr Knightley. Donwell Abbey, one of three houses that dominate the novel, is one mile from Hartfield, which, in turn, is three miles from Randalls, where the Westons live. The village has other identifiable buildings or institutions : the Crown Inn, where Frank Churchill organises the ball; the school, with forty boarders, run by Miss Goddard; and a number of shops, most notably Ford's, 'the principal woollen-draper, linen-draper and haberdasher's shop united', which, according to Mr Weston, 'every body attends every day of their lives'. In one of several scenes at Ford's, Emma, who is waiting while Harriet makes a purchase, goes to the door 'for amusement' :

– Much could not be hoped from the traffic of even the busiest part of Highbury; – Mr Perry walking hastily by, Mr William Cox letting himself in at the office-door, Mr Cole's carriage horses returning from exercise, or a stray letter-boy on an obstinate mule, were the liveliest objects she could presume to expect; and when her eyes fell only on the butcher with his tray, a tidy old woman travelling homewards from shop with her full basket, two curs quarrelling over a dirty bone, and a string of dawling children round the baker's little bow-window eyeing the ginger-bread, she knew she had no reason to complain, and was amused enough; quite enough still to stand at the door. A mind lively and at ease, can do with seeing nothing, and can see nothing that does not answer.

The random details, the local colour, are unusual in Jane Austen, and so, too, is the suggestion of a habit of mind, a way of life, that could find such trivialities sustaining. I'll return to both these points later. At the moment I want to draw attention to certain individuals mentioned here : Mr Perry, William Cox and Mr Cole. The characters actively concerned in the plot of *Emma* number about a dozen – a sizeable and socially varied group. But Jane Austen is concerned to give a fuller sense of Highbury life than a dozen people can provide. She therefore repeatedly reminds the reader of the existence of a large off-stage cast – a cast that includes the three men Emma sees from Ford's. William Cox is mentioned on a number of occasions; he is the 'pert young lawyer' whom Emma briefly considers as a possible suitor for Harriet. Mr Cole, who has made his money in trade, gives a party which Emma unwillingly attends. Hardly a chapter goes by without Mr Perry's name being invoked, but he barely makes a single appearance in the novel. His wife and children, who are frequently referred to, are never seen at all. Other characters lurking in the background are the Martins, Miss Goddard, Miss Nash, Farmer Mitchell, the Gilberts, John Abdy and Mrs Stokes. There is even a sizeable cast of domestic staff : Mr Woodhouse's coachman, James, and his cook, Searle; Mr Knightley's right-hand man, Larkins, and his housekeeper, Mrs Hodges; Miss Bates's Patty, Mrs Elton's Wright.

All these are names that come up more than once, though in some cases at widely scattered intervals. Like the street-names, like the record of distances, they reassure the reader of the range and consistency of Jane Austen's imagination. They show how firmly she is in control of relationships of all kinds in *Emma*. She knows her whole village, and gives it a life of its own, in excess of the demands of her story. Miss Bates, who is first mentioned in Chapter 2, and first described in Chapter 3, does not make her entrance until Chapter 19. In a sense she need never appear. The author clearly knows all about her as she knows all about Mr Perry, and we come to trust the author. *Emma* reads like a transcription of part of a much wider reality. The characters and events described seem to have an existence independent of the written record. It seems appropriate than Jane Austen could tell her family about the death of Mr Woodhouse, two years after Emma's marriage, or the death of Jane Fairfax, nine or ten years after *her* marriage. The story had life beyond the printed page for the author as well as for its readers.

This kind and degree of realism can prompt an over-literal response. There have been attempts to make a map of Highbury, and to prove that it stands for Leatherhead or Cobham. The latter enterprise is doomed, since apparently there could not *be* a village at once sixteen miles from London, nine from Richmond and seven from Box Hill. What this seeming authenticity does usefully prompt in the reader is a tendency to expect and to look for a corresponding scrupulosity in Jane Austen's account of the lives and the social relationships within the village. And this the reader will find. There is a very full sense of the pursuits with which the Highbury people pass their days : gossip, visiting, taking walks, taking tea, music, sketching, riddles, acrostics, cards, backgammon, reading, knitting, carpetwork. The enclosed life of the village is seen to involve an elaborate pattern of small reciprocities. The poor must be visited and given broth. Mrs and Miss Bates must be looked after : if there is a social event in the village, they must be fetched in someone's carriage. Mr Woodhouse must be pampered by his visitors and have a baby-sitter if Emma goes out for the evening. He values the company of Miss Bates because she is 'a great talker upon little matters'. He sends her a leg of pork for a present; Mr Knightley sends a bushel of apples. For a Jane Austen novel *Emma* refers to food with unusual frequency – minced chicken, saddle of mutton, cold lamb, sweetbread, goose, pigeon-pie, boiled eggs, oysters, asparagus, turnip, carrot, parsnips, celery, beetroot, apple-dumplings, tart, cake, custard, walnuts, strawberries. Such viands provide a substantial proportion of the pleasures, the hospitality and the gifts of the community.

Emma's character and conduct are to be judged in terms of this carefully established context of small pleasures and small pains. The circumstantiality doesn't merely provide background – it goes a long way towards defining Emma's very existence. Jane Austen remarks, when her heroine is visiting Randalls :

She could tell nothing of Hartfield, in which Mrs Weston had not a lively concern; and half an hour's uninterrupted communication of all those little matters on which the daily happiness of private life depends, was one of the first gratifications of each.

Emma is vitally concerned with 'those little matters on which the daily happiness of private life depends'. For all Jane Austen's topographical care Highbury is not made particularly visualisable, but it is brought powerfully to life as a social community. It is the antithesis of Gimmerton : the main characters live within it, live by its standards, are defined in relation to it. Much of the effectiveness of the novel, therefore, derives from the skilful realisation of Highbury. The critic who concentrates his attention too exclusively on the leading personalities and the critical episodes of *Emma* is likely to misrepresent the book, to underestimate it.

IV

Hardy's novels, perhaps unexpectedly, provide examples not only of the successful but also of the unsuccessful presentation of place. Little Hintock in *The Woodlanders* is an interestingly defective village. Hardy is specifically concerned with the life and the prospects of a declining community; but he gives the reader no means of knowing how seriously it has declined, or how grave its problems are. Little Hintock is curiously elusive : it has no appearance. If there is such a thing as a village street it is never described. The cottages seem lost among the trees. For all the remoteness of the community it apparently lacks shops or an inn. There is a church, but we never hear of anyone attending it; the vicar is mentioned but never appears. The village would seem to be sparsely populated, since Grace, Giles, and Marty South have not a single friend of their own age; but it is very difficult to decide just how small or how tightly knit the community is. Fitzpiers lives three months in Little Hintock before he meets Giles Winterborne. Although he shares a talkative charwoman with Mr Melbury, it takes him weeks to find out who the newly arrived Grace Melbury can be.

Hardy is even uncharacteristically vague as to distances. Early in the novel Grace Melbury looks out of her window and can dimly discern the outline of Fitzpiers's house among the trees at the top of a hill. Some time later she is shown looking out of the same window. On this occasion she can make out Suke Damson leaving Fitzpiers's house in a night-dress. More surprisingly she sees and recognises Fitzpiers's arm, as it appears round the doorway, and even the sleeve of the dressing-gown surrounding that arm.

Such inconsistencies as these mean that certain aspects of the novel that should be complex are merely confused. To explore Grace Melbury's motives is to waste time. Hardy has in any case awkwardly hedged his bets as to whether the projected marriage between her and Giles derives from an understanding between them or simply from her father's vow; but to leave this point aside hardly helps the case. The past life of Grace and Giles is obscure, because there is no context to define it. Her future existence in Little Hintock, whether as the wife of Winterborne or of Fitzpiers, is similarly unimaginable. How would she pass her days? Who would her friends be? Grace cannot make a meaningful decision about her future life because the alternatives open to her are hopelessly shadowy. Her character is uncertain because the village is uncertain. As a portrayal of a village, of a social community, Little Hintock is a mess. It is the weakness as well as the strength of *The Wood-landers* that the environment which interests Hardy is not the village but the trees.

In a letter to Hardy about *The Mayor of Casterbridge* Robert Louis Stevenson remarks : 'Dorchester is touched in with the hand of a master.' The praise is just. 'Casterbridge' is probably the most fully realised town in English fiction. Perhaps one page in three carries a passage of description or allusion that contributes to the picture. Various streets are named : the High Street, Durnover Hill, West Walk, Bowling Walk, Corn Street. There is a sense of contrasting districts : the Market Place, where much of the action is centred; Mixen Lane, the seedy quarter; Durnover, where the granaries are. A number of descriptions convey an impression of the Casterbridge houses – ancient timbered structures with big bay windows or small lattices. Various landmarks are noted : the grizzled church, the market house, the town pump, the two bridges, the priory mill, the three inns – Peter's Finger, the Three Mariners and the King's Arms. The episodes that make up the novel always take place *somewhere* : the setting is always defined. The first scene inside Casterbridge shows Henchard presiding at the King's Arms. Elizabeth-Jane gets lodgings and work at the Three Mariners, where she meets Farfrae. Henchard meets Susan and later Lucetta at the Roman Ring. The skimmity-ride is planned at Peter's Finger. Casterbridge always dominates the action. The local people are shown working, drinking, gossiping, celebrating. It is to these people, to this environment, that the various newcomers must adapt themselves : Farfrae, Susan, Elizabeth-Jane, Jopp, Lucetta.

An essential aspect of the town is its relationship to the country. One quotation here must do duty for several :

Casterbridge, as has been hinted, was a place deposited in the block upon a corn-field. There was no suburb in the modern sense, or transitional intermixture of town and down. It stood, with regard to the wide fertile land adjoining, clean-cut and distinct, like a chess-board on a green table-cloth. The farmer's boy could sit under his barley-mow and pitch a stone into the office-window of the town-clerk; reapers at work among the sheaves nodded to acquaintances standing on the pavement-corner; the red-robed judge, when he condemned a sheep-stealer, pronounced sentence to the tune of Baa, that floated in at the window from the remainder of the flock browsing hard by; and at executions the waiting crowd stood in a meadow immediately before the drop, out of which the cows had been temporarily driven to give the spectators room.[20]

The stark contiguity of town and country dramatises the direct economic relationship between Casterbridge and the surrounding farms. Hardy's novel is unusual in Victorian fiction in that all the main characters work and are seen to work. Prosperity depends upon their success in pitting their brains, energies and instincts against nature. The reference to the chess-board is not accidental. Earlier the town has been described as being 'compact as a box of dominoes'. Later Hardy remarks that 'a man might gamble upon the square green areas of fields as readily as upon those of a card-room'. For corn-dealers, such as Henchard and Farfrae, each harvest is a contest, a battle of wits. The metaphors from games and gambling are barely metaphorical; they suggest pretty exactly the predicament of Casterbridge at a period when 'A bad harvest, or the prospect of one, would double the price of corn in a few weeks; and the promise of a good yield would lower it as rapidly'. The story Hardy tells is intrinsic to the town he describes, with its precarious dependence on the countryside and the weather. Even the characters derive partly from these conditions. The fatalism, the stoicism, the superstitiousness are all nurtured by the environment.

Casterbridge is first seen from the outside, as it appears to 'the level eye' of Elizabeth-Jane on her arrival; but Hardy cuts quickly to a different view :

To birds of the more soaring kind Casterbridge must have appeared on this fine evening as a mosaic-work of subdued reds, browns, greys, and crystals, held together by a rectangular frame of deep green.

It would never have occurred to Jane Austen to give a bird's-eye view of Highbury. Later Hardy goes underground :

> Casterbridge announced old Rome in every street, alley, and precinct. It looked Roman, bespoke the art of Rome, concealed dead men of Rome. It was impossible to dig more than a foot or two deep about the town fields and gardens without coming upon some tall soldier or other of the Empire, who had lain there in his silent unobtrusive rest for a space of fifteen hundred years. He was mostly found lying on his side, in an oval scoop in the chalk, like a chicken in its shell. . . .

The soaring bird and the dead Roman enable the reader to glimpse Casterbridge from extreme perspectives of distance and time. For an instant the town that so vividly surrounds and contains the action of the novel recedes almost to vanishing-point. Such shifts are frequent in Hardy : it is his habit to reduce his leading characters, from time to time, to mere specks in history or in a landscape. The annihilating effect is redressed by his converse sense of the importance and the complexity of the individual personality. But between these extremes social life can go for nothing, as in Little Hintock, where there are people and trees, but there is no village. Hardy's developed portrayal of the town in *The Mayor of Casterbridge* gives him an unusual degree of control over his shifts of perspective. As his title implies, he is describing an established structured community, with traditions, a way of life, a hierarchy. It is this multi-dimensional society, within which the individual dramas are enacted, that is put into relationship with the adjacent countryside and with its own past history.

As with Highbury the authenticity of the description is an invitation to map-making. But in this case a map not only can, but does, surely, exist – the map of Dorchester. The two towns match in all essentials. More than that : in a preface Hardy refers to 'the real history of the town called Casterbridge'; in a footnote to a description of Casterbridge High Street he comments, 'Most of these old houses have now been pulled down (1912)'. The implication must be that Casterbridge *is* Dorchester. But when Hardy was made an honorary freeman of Dorchester, years after writing *The Mayor of Casterbridge*, he made a speech on the matter that was characteristically wary and ambiguous :

> . . . when I consider the liberties I have taken with its ancient walls, streets, and precincts through the medium of the printing-

press, I feel that I have treated its external features with the hand of freedom indeed. True, it might be urged that my Casterbridge (if I may mention seriously a name coined off-hand in a moment with no thought of its becoming established and localised) is not Dorchester – not even the Dorchester as it existed sixty years ago, but a dream-place that never was outside an irresponsible book. Nevertheless, when somebody said to me that 'Casterbridge' is a sort of essence of the town as it used to be, 'a place more Dorchester than Dorchester itself', I could not absolutely contradict him, though I could not quite perceive it. At any rate, it is not a photograph in words, that inartistic species of literary produce. . . .

The seemingly contradictory nature of these comments reflects a genuine difficulty of definition. Building for building, street for street, the two towns may seem to correspond; but Hardy was left free to select, to concentrate, to omit. The town he imagined could have differed from the Dorchester he knew. And in any case the Dorchester which Casterbridge represented would have had to be a Dorchester which he had never seen, because it existed before he was born. No one suggests that Henchard and Farfrae, or specific models for them, were actual mayors of Dorchester : Hardy's story is fiction, not fictionalised history. His use of Dorchester as a model for Casterbridge draws that fiction into an intriguingly close alignment with actuality, but the gap between the two remains absolute.

V

The great nineteenth-century novelists annexed new territory to fiction in an almost literal sense : Scotland, Wessex, the Yorkshire moors. In our age of easy travel and communication we tend to forget how much pleasure readers must have found in encountering unfamiliar places and people. The distances to be travelled could be social rather than geographical. *Sketches by Boz* makes it clear that enormous areas of London were unknown to most of Dickens's audience. He writes like an explorer or an anthropologist, clearly assuming that even those who have visited Monmouth Street or Seven Dials will not really have *seen* those places, have understood them for what they are. He has a powerful sense of the identity and flavour of a district. The London of the early novels is very much made up of set-piece descriptions. In *Nicholas Nickleby*, for example, Dickens makes occasion to describe Golden Square, Manchester Buildings, Snow Hill, Cadogan Place. Some of these passages are excellent in themselves, but they tend to read like interpolations. They aren't sufficiently *used*; they don't inform the narrative to any significant extent. Clearly it wasn't easy for Dickens to adapt his mode of seeing and describing London to the requirements of fiction.

Gissing was to have a simpler task, because although he knew London so well he saw far less, and seems to have had no great feeling for particular localities. The streets and districts he is at pains to specify serve chiefly to define social status and physical movement. In *New Grub Street* every major character has an address, or even a series of addresses. Reardon starts his London career in a street parallel to Tottenham Court Road, moves to Regent's Park when he marries, and later declines to a garret in Manville Street, off Upper Street, in Islington. Biffen lives first in Clipstone Street and later in Goodge Street. Milvain progresses from Mornington Road, near Camden Town, to Bayswater; and Whelpdale from Albany Street to Earl's Court. Amy Reardon's parents live in Westbourne Park; Marian Yule lives in St Paul's Crescent, Camden Town. Much of the social definition, of course, has been lost. The area with which Gissing is chiefly concerned in this novel, an area stretching from Regent's Park and Camden Town along Hampstead Road and Tottenham Court Road towards the British Museum, has lately been drastically altered by rebuilding, rerouting and gentrification. Biffen's lodgings in Clipstone Street would now be in the shadow of the Post Office tower. Even when the book was first published it could have been fully appreciated only by the north-Londoner. A Mancunian, say, could have had little feeling either for the localities Gissing mentions or for the topographical relationships that he stresses.

> They issued into Clipstone Street, turned northward, crossed Euston Road, and came into Albany Street. . . .
>
> Down Pentonville Hill, up Euston Road, all along Marylebone Road, then northwestwards towards the point of his destination.
>
> . . . he struck across Kensington Gardens, and then on towards Fulham, where he crossed the Thames to Putney.

As a Londoner I enjoy such passages; mainly, I think, for two reasons. The familiar names are evocative, and when strung together like this have an odd poetic suggestiveness which cannot easily be accounted for. Harold Pinter carries this effect to its limit in *The Caretaker*, where one long speech is a litany of London bus routes and destinations.[21] My other pleasure is also a very abstract one. Because the streets and journeys Gissing mentions exist in my real world as well as in his novel they constitute something like a trick of perspective. It is as though I could walk down Euston Road into the pages of *New Grub Street*. But is either of these responses accessible to the Mancunian who knows nothing of the districts concerned? Would a comparable account of Manchester streets have any meaning for me?

What might be conveyed, in either case, is a sense of imaginative fullness and solidity. The characters in Gissing's novels move around a good deal – in particular, they walk a good deal – and he always knows where they are going and what route they will take. The precision about distances interacts with a comparable precision about money, clothes and food to produce an extreme sharpness of definition in many of the episodes in his novels. Reardon's visit to his estranged wife proves disastrous partly because his clothes are so shabby, but partly because of the effect on his mood and his appearance of a rainy six-mile walk from Upper Street to West-bourne Park. Gissing's knowledge of London seems to give him imaginative security. Much of the action of *Thyrza* takes place in Lambeth, and most of the leading characters live in actual streets that are very close together: Paradise Street, Newport Street, Kennington Road, Lambeth Walk. The real-life location seems to serve as an armature for Gissing's story-telling. He achieves by a short cut a kind of assurance that some novelists lack altogether and some only achieve through sustained imaginative effort. His characters are placed, topographically. He knows, say, that if his heroine is to visit her lover she will turn left at her front door. Such knowledge can in some sense be communicated to the reader even where the streets are imaginary – even, perhaps, where the details of place and distance don't appear in the text. The reader comes to feel that the novelist knows where he is and where his characters are, that one imaginative dimension is secure.

Dickens learns to use London backgrounds to somewhat similar effect. Only by walking over the ground can one get a full sense of the contiguity of Lincoln's Inn (home of the Court of Chancery, and of the offices of Kenge & Carboy), Lincoln's Inn Fields (where Mr Tulkinghorn lives), Chichester Rents (where Krook has his warehouse) and Cursitor Street (the site of Coavinses). Dickens seems to take his terrain so much for granted that he only occasionally spells out relationships in a Gissing-like way, as when Guppy describes the route from Mr Kenge's office to the Jellybys' house in Thavies Inn: 'We just twist up Chancery Lane, and cut along

Holborn, and there we are in four minutes' time, as near as a
toucher.' But these relationships permeate *Bleak House* – almost
constitute the subject of the novel. Within this little enclave of the
Law the victimisers and the victimised, the rich and the poor, the
administrators and the executants live side by side. The obvious
contrasts and discrepancies, the hidden similarities and mutual
dependence are a type of those in society at large. Dickens investi-
gates the condition of England by exploring the area round
Lincoln's Inn.

Ultimately this kind of response to London is very different from
Gissing's, despite the superficial resemblance. A passage from *Oliver
Twist* will illustrate one kind of divergence. Bill Sikes is taking
Oliver across London on the way to a robbery :

> Turning down Sun Street and Crown Street, and crossing Fins-
> bury Square, Mr Sikes struck, by way of Chiswell Street, into
> Barbican : thence into Long Lane, and so into Smithfield; from
> which latter place arose a tumult of discordant sounds that filled
> Oliver Twist with amazement.

So far the account is Gissingesque. The route is described in detail,
and could be followed on a map, or on foot. But with the final clause
the emphasis is beginning to shift; and the succeeding paragraph
shifts it much farther :

> It was market-morning. The ground was covered, nearly ankle-
> deep, with filth and mire; a thick steam, perpetually rising from
> the reeking bodies of the cattle, and mingling with the fog, which
> seemed to rest upon the chimney-tops, hung heavily above. . . .
> Countrymen, butchers, drovers, hawkers, boys, thieves, idlers, and
> vagabonds of every low grade, were mingled together in a mass;
> the whistling of drovers, the barking of dogs, the bellowing and
> plunging of oxen, the bleating of sheep, the grunting and squeak-
> ing of pigs, the cries of hawkers, the shouts, oaths, and quarrelling
> on all sides; the ringing of bells and roar of voices . . . rendered
> it a stunning and bewildering scene, which quite confounded the
> senses.

It isn't merely that Dickens has shifted from itinerary to description:
this is description of a highly subjective kind. We are made to
experience the market through Oliver's senses. The account of
Smithfield is really an account of Oliver's state of mind as he is led
through a strange city on a sinister errand, frightened, confused,
disorientated. Smithfield Market is no doubt disagreeable in itself,

but we respond to this passage as a projection of Oliver's feelings rather than as a description of an actual scene. Smithfield is to Oliver as Salisbury is to Tom Pinch.

But many of Dickens's descriptions of London, though similarly heightened, function in a quite different way – almost in the reverse way. The intensity of feeling is not projected from without but generated by the scene itself :

> The mud lay thick upon the stones, and a black mist hung over the streets; the rain fell sluggishly down, and everything felt cold and clammy to the touch. It seemed just the night when it befitted such a being as the Jew to be abroad. As he glided stealthily along, creeping beneath the shelter of the walls and doorways, the hideous old man seemed like some loathsome reptile, engendered in the slime and darkness through which he moved : crawling forth, by night, in search of some rich offal for a meal.

This is not a subjective description in the conventional sense. From two points of view the word 'engendered' is more than a metaphor. The poverty, the dirt, the ugliness breed crime. In *Nicholas Nickleby* the descriptions of London are merely decorative, because the novel is not about *Londoners*; but Fagin is a child of Saffron Hill as Jo is a child of Tom-all-Alone's. Dickens does not deform the background as a means of commenting on his character : the character is an expression of that background. The place came first. Saffron Hill can also be said to have 'engendered' Fagin in that it is Dickens's intense response to the atmosphere of the district that begets a Fagin, or a Sikes, or an Artful Dodger. Gissing's London is little more than a map – though a very detailed map, very effectively used. Dickens does not merely know London well : he sees it and experiences it so vividly that his accounts of the city slip naturally and imperceptibly from realism into expressionism.

VI

This book has been concerned with the realistic novel, and its essential theme has been relationship. Realism implies relationship, relativity. If the various phenomena described are not shown to be connected in some way the result will be not art, but miscellaneousness. The reader of a novel may ask, concerning any given descriptive detail : 'Why is it included? If it is relevant, how is it relevant?' The realist writer is constantly implying positive answers to such questions. The account of a character's face may reveal his personality; his clothes may establish his social status; his house may display his values. As D. H. Lawrence claimed : 'The novel is the highest form of subtle inter-relatedness that man has discovered.' In the ideal realistic narrative nothing could be redundant; the smallest element would somehow reinforce or modify the rest.

To proceed to further chapters on landscape and weather would take me to a different category of relationship : that between Man and Nature, or Man and God. It might be appropriate to stop at the attempt to realise a village, a town, a community, because that attempt is the extreme exercise in the kind of inter-connectedness that I have been trying to illustrate. It is an audacious enterprise. Within this very selective chapter I have mentioned techniques for conveying some sense of a town's traditions, of its architecture, of its topography, of its atmosphere, of its work, of its domestic life, of its social activity, of its climate of opinion, of its liability to change. What novelist could hope to comprehend all these aspects of a community's existence within a single narrative? And, if he must leave gaps, how is he to disguise them?

It seems to me that many students, and some critics, too easily take for granted the extraordinary attempt by the great nineteenth-century novelists to construct art from the manifold circumstances and contingencies of everyday life. An enormous range of phenomena and kinds of phenomena had somehow to be defined, placed, proportioned. The writer needed remarkable resources of intellectual and imaginative energy, of stamina, of technique. There was always a strong possibility that his narrative would lead him into areas in which his judgment, his experience, or his descriptive skills would prove insufficient. Notoriously Dickens fails with his heroines, Hardy with his intellectuals, Eliot with her Jews. But there is something admirable in the very willingness of these authors to court such risks. Their work had breadth and freedom. In many contemporary novels the writer's various 'meanings' are confined and circumscribed by some thesis or formal stratagem. Narrative and description go only where they are allowed to go. There is little danger of miscalculation, imbalance, redundancy, self-contradiction. The typical Victorian novel requires you to look for significance in terms of a slowly emerging pattern of relationships between an immense variety of elements, some important, some trivial, some the product of the intellect, some of imaginative instinct. It says more because it contains more. The author may fall short of his conscious purpose, but he may also exceed it. In showing how he looks at the world about him he is likely to betray limitations and prejudices – who would not? But he also projects a view of life.

Notes

CHAPTER 2

1 Michael Frayn, *The Tin Men* (London, 1965), pp. 117–18.
2 E. H. Gombrich, *Art and Illusion* (London, 1962), p. 148.
3 ibid., p. 185.
4 ibid., p. 182.
5 ibid., p. 184.
6 ibid., p. 174.
7 Anton Chekhov, *Plays,* trans. Elizaveta Fen (Penguin, Harmondsworth, 1959), p. 177. Cf. Avrahm Yarmolinsky (ed.), *Letters of Anton Chekhov* (London, 1974), p. 37.
8 Quotations from the Penguin edition (Harmondsworth, 1954), trans. Rosemary Edmonds.
9 Florence Emily Hardy, *The Life of Thomas Hardy,* 1840–1928 (London, 1962), p. 260.
10 John Carey, *The Violent Effigy* (London, 1973), p. 61.

CHAPTER 3

11 Erving Goffman, *Relations in Public* (London, 1971), pp. 200–1.
12 F. R. and Q. D. Leavis, *Dickens the Novelist* (London, 1970), p. 262.
13 Barbara Hardy, *The Moral Art of Dickens* (Oxford, 1970), pp. 139*ff*.
14 Morris Shapira (ed.), *Henry James: Selected Literary Criticism* (Harmondsworth, 1968), p. 63.
15 F. R. Leavis, *The Great Tradition* (London, 1948), p. 102.
16 David Cecil, *Early Victorian Novelists* (London, 1934), p. 27.
17 F. R. and Q. D. Leavis, *Dickens the Novelist,* p. 87.

CHAPTER 5

18 Penguin edition, trans. Rosemary Edmonds, p. 48.

CHAPTER 6

19 Anthony Trollope, *An Autobiography* (Oxford, 1950), p. 154.
20 *The Life of Thomas Hardy,* op. cit., p. 351.
21 Harold Pinter, *The Caretaker* (London, 1960), p. 34.

Index